D1482125

SHAKESPEARE

ROMEO AND
JULIET

REVIEW QUESTIONS AND ANSWERS

COLES EDITORIAL BOARD

ABOUT COLES NOTES

COLES NOTES have been an indispensible aid to students on five continents since 1948.

COLES NOTES are available for a wide range of individual literary works. Clear, concise explanations and insights are provided along with interesting interpretations and evaluations.

Proper use of COLES NOTES will allow the student to pay greater attention to lectures and spend less time taking notes. This will result in a broader understanding of the work being studied and will free the student for increased participation in discussions.

COLES NOTES are an invaluable aid for review and exam preparation as well as an invitation to explore different interpretive paths.

COLES NOTES are written by experts in their fields. It should be noted that any literary judgement expressed herein is just that – the judgement of one school of thought. Interpretations that diverge from, or totally disagree with any criticism may be equally valid.

COLES NOTES are designed to supplement the text and are not intended as a substitute for reading the text itself. Use of the NOTES will serve not only to clarify the work being studied, but should enhance the readers enjoyment of the topic.

ISBN 0-7740-2938-2

Copyright 2009 and Published by
Coles Publishing
A division of Prospero Books
Toronto Canada
Publisher: Indigo Books and Music Inc.

Designed and Printed in Canada

Printed on Legacy Book Opaque 100%, manufactured from
100% post-consumer waste and is FSC-certified.
Manufacturing this book in Canada ensures compliance with strict
environmental practices and eliminates the need for international freight
shipping, a major contributor to global and air pollution.
Manufactured by Webcom

CONTENTS

Part A: The Play in Brief

Introduction

As enjoyable and important as Shakespeare's plays are, they can be difficult to read. Since Shakespeare wrote his plays to appeal to Elizabethan audiences, much of the text is dated and means little to the average reader of today.

We are, therefore, presenting the substance of the play in readable form by eliminating, as much as possible, the outdated passages and by paraphrasing the more complicated ones. This will give you a better understanding and appreciation of the play, and will make the questions and answers more meaningful.

CHARACTERS IN THE PLAY

Escalus: Prince of Verona.

Paris: A young count; relative of the prince.

Montague } Heads of two warring households.
Capulet }

An Old Man: Member of Capulet family.

Romeo: Montague's son.

Mercutio: Relative of the prince and friend of Romeo.

Benvolio: Montague's nephew and Romeo's friend.

Tybalt: Lady Capulet's nephew.

Friar Laurence } Franciscans.
Friar John }

Balthasar: Romeo's servant.

Sampson } Capulet's servants.
Gregory }

Peter: Servant of Juliet's nurse.

Abraham: Montague's servant.

An Apothecary

Three Musicians

An Officer

Lady Montague: Montague's wife.

Lady Capulet: Capulet's wife.

Juliet: Capulet's daughter.

Nurse

Citizens of Verona, Gentlemen and Gentlewomen of two households, Maskers, Torchbearers, Guards, Pages, Watchmen, Servants and Attendants.

Chorus

ACT I

A prologue in sonnet form opens *Romeo and Juliet*:

Two households, both alike in dignity,
In fair Verona, where we lay our scene,
From ancient grudge break to new mutiny,
Where civil blood makes civil hands unclean.
From forth the fatal loins of these two foes
A pair of star-cross'd lovers take their life;
Whose misadventured piteous overthrows
Do with their death bury their parents' strife.
The fearful passage of their death-mark'd love,
And the continuance of their parents' rage,
Which, but their children's end, nought could remove,
Is now the two hours' traffic of our stage;
The which if you with patient ears attend,
What here shall miss, our toil shall strive to mend.

The feud between the two great Veronese families, Montague and Capulet, extends even to the servants of the two houses, and the action of the drama begins with a street fight started by four servants, two from each of the warring households. Benvolio, a relative of Romeo and a Montague, attempts to stop it, but Tybalt, Juliet's hot-tempered cousin and a Capulet, enrages him, and they also fight. Others take sides, and the noise attracts Lord and Lady Montague and Lord and Lady Capulet. Capulet and Montague are anxious to join in the fight and do their share, but the ladies try to restrain their husbands. The prince comes to put a stop to the fight. There have been other outbreaks before this, and he must deal strictly with the offenders:

If ever you disturb our streets again,
Your lives shall pay the forfeit of the peace.
For this time, all the rest depart away:
You, Capulet, shall go along with me;
And, Montague, come you this afternoon,
To know our further pleasure in this case,
To old Free-town, our common judgement-place.
Once more, on pain of death, all men depart.

Everyone leaves except Montague, his lady and Benvolio.

Old Montague listens to Benvolio's story of this latest brawl. Lady Montague is relieved that her son, Romeo, was not present, and asks Benvolio whether Romeo has been seen recently. Benvolio replies:

> Madam, an hour before the worshipp'd sun
> Peer'd forth the golden window of the east,
> A troubled mind drave me to walk abroad;
> Where, underneath the grove of sycamore
> That westward rooteth from the city's side,
> So early walking did I see your son:
> Towards him I made; but he was ware of me,
> And stole into the covert of the wood:
> I, measuring his affections by my own,
> Which then most sought where most might not be
> found,
> Being one too many by my weary self,
> Pursued my humour, not pursuing his,
> And gladly shunn'd who gladly fled from me.

Montague comments further upon Romeo's strange behavior recently:

> Many a morning hath he there been seen,
> With tears augmenting the fresh morning's dew,
> Adding to clouds more clouds with his deep sighs:
> But all so soon as the all-cheering sun
> Should in the farthest east begin to draw
> The shady curtains from Aurora's bed,
> Away from light steals home my heavy son,
> And private in his chamber pens himself,
> Shuts up his windows, locks fair daylight out,
> And makes himself an artificial night:
> Black and portentous must this humour prove,
> Unless good counsel may the cause remove.

Neither Montague nor Benvolio knows the cause of Romeo's apparent misery, and Montague's efforts to learn more about his son's problems have been unsuccessful:

> Both by myself and many other friends:
> But he, his own affections' counsellor,

3

Is to himself—I will not say how true—
But to himself so secret and so close,
So far from sounding and discovery,
As is the bud bit with an envious worm,
Ere he can spread his sweet leaves to the air,
Or dedicate his beauty to the sun.
Could we but learn from whence his sorrows grow,
We would as willingly give cure as know.

At this moment, Romeo appears, and Benvolio tells
Montague and Lady Montague that, if they will leave him with
Romeo, he will try to find out his trouble. When they have gone,
Benvolio questions Romeo and finds out that he is in love with a
lady who does not return his affection. Romeo says:

She will not stay the siege of loving terms,
Nor bide the encounter of assailing eyes,
Nor ope her lap to saint-seducing gold:
O, she is rich in beauty, only poor
That, when she dies, with beauty dies her store.
Benvolio: Then she hath sworn that she will still live
chaste?
Romeo: She hath, and in that sparing makes huge
waste;
For beauty, starved with her severity,
Cuts beauty off from all posterity.
She is too fair, too wise, wisely too fair,
To merit bliss by making me despair:
She hath forsworn to love; and in that vow
Do I live dead, that live to tell it now.

Benvolio advises Romeo to forget about this woman "By
giving liberty unto thine eyes;/Examine other beauties." But
Romeo protests that he cannot forget her:

He that is strucken blind cannot forget
The precious treasure of his eyesight lost:

A short time later, Capulet and Paris, a young nobleman,
meet on the street and discuss the prince's judgment on the
recent feud. Both wish for an end to the ancient quarrel. Paris

then turns the conversation to his desire to marry Juliet. Capulet reminds Paris that Juliet is only 14, too young to think of marriage yet. But Paris is impatient, and Capulet advises him:

> But woo her, gentle Paris, get her heart;
> My will to her consent is but a part;
> An she agree, within her scope of choice
> Lies my consent and fair according voice.
> This night I hold an old accustom'd feast,
> Whereto I have invited many a guest,
> Such as I love; and you among the store,
> One more, most welcome, makes my number more.
> At my poor house look to behold this night
> Earth-treading stars that make dark heaven light:
> Such comfort as do lusty young men feel
> When well-apparell'd April on the heel
> Of limping winter treads, even such delight
> Among fresh female buds shall you this night
> Inherit at my house; hear all, all see,
> And like her most whose merit most shall be:
> Which on more view, of many mine being one
> May stand in number, though in reckoning none.

Capulet then hands a servant a paper containing the list of guests and sends him to invite each one to a masked ball that is being held that night. Unfortunately, the servant cannot read, so he seeks help from the first passers-by, who happen to be Benvolio and Romeo. Benvolio is giving further advice to Romeo about his love affair:

> Tut, man, one fire burns out another's burning.
>   One pain is lessen'd by another's anguish;
> Turn giddy, and be holp by backward turning;
>   One desperate grief cures with another's languish:
> Take thou some new infection to thy eye,
> And the rank poison of the old will die.

The servant interrupts them to ask Romeo to read his list for him. Thus, they learn of the party. A brilliant idea occurs to Benvolio:

5

At this same ancient feast of Capulet's
Sups the fair Rosaline whom thou so lovest,
With all the admired beauties of Verona:
Go thither, and with unattainted eye
Compare her face with some that I shall show,
And I will make thee think thy swan a crow.

Romeo is shocked by Benvolio's suggestion that Rosaline could be considered anything but beautiful, even compared to all the "admired beauties of Verona." Romeo defends the holiness of his love:

When the devout religion of mine eye
Maintains such falsehood, then turn tears to fires;
And these, who, often drown'd, could never die,
    Transparent heretics, be burnt for liars!
One fairer than my love! the all-seeing sun
Ne'er saw her match since first the world begun.

However, Romeo agrees to attend the feast just to see Rosaline.
Before the party, Juliet must be told about Paris' marriage proposal. Lady Capulet sends Juliet's nurse to call the girl. When Juliet appears, Lady Capulet and the nurse begin to discuss Juliet's age. In a long speech, the nurse recalls how her dead daughter, Susan, and Juliet were born on the same day and how Juliet was weaned on the day of an earthquake. The nurse takes great pleasure in repeating her husband's sexual joke on that occasion:

'Yea,' quoth he, 'dost thou fall upon thy face?
Thou wilt fall backward when thou hast more wit;
Wilt thou not, Jule?' and, by my halidom,
The pretty wretch left crying, and said 'Ay.'

The nurse dwells on this coarse remark until both Lady Capulet and Juliet tell her to be quiet. The nurse cannot resist making one more affectionate remark about young Juliet:

Peace, I have done. God mark thee to his grace!
Thou wast the prettiest babe that e'er I nursed:
An I might live to see thee married once,
I have my wish.

This reference to marriage is just the lead for which Lady Capulet has been waiting. She turns to Juliet and asks her what she thinks about marriage. Juliet replies that it is an honor she does not dream of. Then her mother tells her about Paris:

> Well, think of marriage now; younger than you
> Here in Verona, ladies of esteem,
> Are made already mothers. By my count,
> I was your mother much upon these years
> That you are now a maid. Thus then in brief;
> The valiant Paris seeks you for his love.

He is to be at the feast at their home that night, and there Juliet may see him. Juliet replies obediently, but cautiously:

> I'll look to like, if looking liking move:
> But no more deep will I endart mine eye
> Than your consent gives strength to make it fly.

Satisfied with this response, Lady Capulet goes to greet their guests.

By this time, it is evening. Romeo, Mercutio and Benvolio, along with other maskers, are on their way to the Capulets' feast. Unexpected guests at a feast were expected to apologize for their visit and then do a dance, or "measure," while others held torches to show off the performance. Romeo, however, insists that he is too heartbroken to dance; he will only hold a torch. The others tease Romeo about his lovesick attitude, and Mercutio reveals his cynical, mocking view of love by speaking in sexual puns that stress the physical side of love. When Romeo regrets that love "is too rough, / Too rude, too boisterous, and it pricks like a thorn," Mercutio casually replies, "If love be rough with you, be rough with love;/ Prick love for pricking, and you beat love down."

Romeo then reveals his fear of attending the feast because of a dream he has had. Romeo's mention of this dream leads Mercutio to suggest, in one of the most famous speeches of the play, that Romeo has been visited by fairies:

> O, then, I see Queen Mab hath been with you.
> She is the fairies' midwife, and she comes

In shape no bigger than an agate-stone
On the fore-finger of an alderman,
Drawn with a team of little atomies
Athwart men's noses as they lie asleep:
Her waggon-spokes made of long spinners' legs;
The cover, of the wings of grasshoppers;
Her traces, of the smallest spider's web;
Her collars, of the moonshine's watery beams;
Her whip, of cricket's bone; the lash, of film;
Her waggoner, a small grey-coated gnat,
Not half so big as a round little worm
Prick'd from the lazy finger of a maid:
Her chariot is an empty hazel-nut,
Made by the joiner squirrel or old grub,
Time out o' mind the fairies' coachmakers.
And in this state she gallops night by night
Through lovers' brains, and then they dream of love;
O'er courtiers' knees, that dream on court'sies straight;
O'er lawyers' fingers, who straight dream on fees;
O'er ladies' lips, who straight on kisses dream,
Which oft the angry Mab with blisters plagues,
Because their breaths with sweetmeats tainted are:
Sometime she gallops o'er a courtier's nose,
And then dreams he of smelling out a suit;
And sometime comes she with a tithe-pig's tail
Tickling a parson's nose as a' lies asleep,
Then dreams he of another benefice:
Sometime she driveth o'er a soldier's neck,
And then dreams he of cutting foreign throats,
Of breaches, ambuscadoes, Spanish blades,
Of healths five fathom deep; and then anon
Drums in his ear, at which he starts and wakes,
And being thus frighted swears a prayer or two,
And sleeps again. This is that very Mab
That plats the manes of horses in the night,
And bakes the elf-locks in foul sluttish hairs,
Which once untangled much misfortune bodes:
This is the hag, when maids lie on their backs,
That presses them and learns them first to bear,
Making them women of good carriage:

Romeo begs Mercutio to stop: "Thou talkst of nothing." Mercutio answers, "True, I talk of dreams,/Which are the children of an idle brain/Begot of nothing but vain fantasy." But Romeo misses the significance of Mercutio's remarks. When Benvolio attempts to hurry them on to the feast, Romeo suddenly senses disaster approaching:

I fear, too early: for my mind misgives
Some consequence, yet hanging in the stars,
Shall bitterly begin his fearful date
With this night's revels, and expire the term
Of a despised life closed in my breast,
By some vile forfeit of untimely death:
But He, that hath the steerage of my course,
Direct my sail! On, lusty gentlemen.

The servants are still preparing for the dance as Romeo, Benvolio and Mercutio arrive. Old Capulet, Juliet and others meet the maskers as they enter. The old man gives them a hearty welcome and calls upon the musicians to play and the guests to dance, at the same time talking busily with an old cousin of his about the 25 or 30 years that have passed since they last danced. Romeo, meanwhile, has stood watching the guests and finally speaks to a nearby servant:

What lady's that, which doth enrich the hand
Of yonder knight?
Servingman: I know not, sir.
Romeo: O, she doth teach the torches to burn bright!
It seems she hangs upon the cheek of night
Like a rich jewel in an Ethiop's ear;
Beauty too rich for use, for earth too dear!
So shows a snowy dove trooping with crows,
As yonder lady o'er her fellows shows.
The measure done, I'll watch her place of
stand,
And, touching hers, make blessed my rude
hand.
Did my heart love till now? forswear it, sight!
For I ne'er saw true beauty till this night.

Tybalt overhears Romeo talking to himself. He thinks the speaker is a Montague and prepares to challenge him. But old Capulet puts a stop to such action. He says it is no way to treat a guest:

Content thee, gentle coz, let him alone,
He bears him like a portly gentleman;
And, to say truth, Verona brags of him
To be a virtuous and well-govern'd youth:
I would not for the wealth of all this town
Here in my house do him disparagement:
Therefore be patient, take no note of him:
It is my will, the which if thou respect,
Show a fair presence and put off these frowns.

Romeo, who has been intent upon Juliet, now speaks to her:

If I profane with my unworthiest hand
    This holy shrine, the gentle fine is this,
My lips, two blushing pilgrims, ready stand
    To smooth that rough touch with a tender kiss.
Juliet: Good pilgrim, you do wrong your hand too much,
    Which mannerly devotion shows in this;
For saints have hands that pilgrims' hands do touch,
    And palm to palm is holy palmers' kiss.
Romeo: Have not saints lips, and holy palmers too?
Juliet: Ay, pilgrim, lips that they must use in prayer.
Romeo: O, then, dear saint, let lips do what hands do;
They pray, grant thou, lest faith turn to despair.
Juliet: Saints do not move, though grant for prayers' sake.
Romeo: Then move not, while my prayer's effect I take.
Thus from my lips by thine my sin is purged.
                                            [*Kissing her*]
Juliet: Then have my lips the sin that they have took.
Romeo: Sin from my lips? O trespass sweetly urged!
Give me my sin again.
Juliet: You kiss by the book.

The nurse interrupts this romantic exchange when she comes to tell Juliet that Lady Capulet, who probably has been watching the young couple, wishes to speak to her daughter. When Juliet is gone, Romeo asks the nurse, "What is her mother?" Learning that Juliet is a Capulet, Romeo cries, "O dear account! My life is my foe's debt."

As the party is ending, Juliet sends the nurse to find out about Romeo. "If he be married," Juliet fears, "My grave is like to be my wedding bed." When the nurse returns with the information that Romeo is a Montague, Juliet exclaims:

My only love sprung from my only hate!
Too early seen unknown, and known too late!
Prodigious birth of love it is to me,
That I must love a loathed enemy.

ACT II

Another prologue introduces this act:

Now old desire doth in his death-bed lie,
    And young affection gapes to be his heir;
That fair for which love groan'd for and would die,
    With tender Juliet match'd, is now not fair.
Now Romeo is beloved and loves again,
    Alike bewitched by the charm of looks,
But to his foe supposed he must complain,
    And she steal love's sweet bait from fearful hooks:
Being held a foe, he may not have access
    To breathe such vows as lovers use to swear;
And she as much in love, her means much less
    To meet her new beloved any where:
But passion lends them power, time means, to meet,
Tempering extremities with extreme sweet.

Romeo appears in a lane by Capulet's orchard and climbs the wall surrounding it. As he leaps down into the orchard, Benvolio and Mercutio appear, hunting for him. Benvolio has seen Romeo climb the wall, so Mercutio calls to him and dares him to answer by Rosaline's bright eyes. Mercutio then teases Romeo by, again, using crude sexual word play. Benvolio warns Mercutio to stop before he angers Romeo. His love is blind, says Benvolio, and he seeks the dark for comfort. But there is no response from Romeo, and his two friends give up the search and go away.

On the orchard side of the wall, Romeo speaks:

He jests at scars that never felt a wound.
                    [*Juliet appears above at a window*]
But, soft! what light through yonder window breaks?
It is the east, and Juliet is the sun!
Arise, fair sun, and kill the envious moon,
Who is already sick and pale with grief,
That thou her maid art far more fair than she:
Be not her maid, since she is envious;
Her vestal livery is but sick and green,
And none but fools do wear it; cast it off.
It is my lady; O, it is my love!

O, that she knew she were!
She speaks, yet she says nothing: what of that?
Her eye discourses, I will answer it.
I am too bold, 'tis not to me she speaks:
Two of the fairest stars in all the heaven,
Having some business, do intreat her eyes
To twinkle in their spheres till they return.
What if her eyes were there, they in her head?
The brightness of her cheek would shame those stars,
As daylight doth a lamp; her eyes in heaven
Would through the airy region stream so bright
That birds would sing and think it were not night.
See, how she leans her cheek upon her hand!
O, that I were a glove upon that hand,
That I might touch that cheek!

Juliet sighs, and Romeo, hearing the sound of her voice, is
anxious for her to say more:

O, speak again, bright angel! for thou art
As glorious to this night, being o'er my head,
As is a winged messenger of heaven
Unto the white-upturned wondering eyes
Of mortals that fall back to gaze on him,
When he bestrides the lazy-pacing clouds
And sails upon the bosom of the air.

Still unaware of Romeo's presence, Juliet continues:

O Romeo, Romeo! wherefore art thou Romeo?
Deny thy father and refuse thy name;
Or, if thou wilt not, be but sworn my love
And I'll no longer be a Capulet.
Romeo: [*Aside*] Shall I hear more, or shall I speak at
this?
Juliet: 'Tis but thy name that is my enemy;
Thou art thyself, though not a Montague.
What's Montague? it is nor hand, nor foot,
Nor arm, nor face, nor any other part
Belonging to a man. O, be some other name!
What's in a name? that which we call a rose

13

By any other name would smell as sweet;
As Romeo would, were he not Romeo call'd,
Retain that dear perfection which he owes
Without that title. Romeo, doff thy name,
And for thy name, which is no part of thee,
Take all myself.

At this point, Romeo announces his presence. Startled by Romeo's sudden appearance, Juliet asks how he came to this place. Romeo replies:

With love's light wings did I o'er-perch these walls,
For stony limits cannot hold love out:
And what love can do, that dares love attempt;
Therefore thy kinsmen are no let to me.

Romeo also tells Juliet that he found his way:

By love, that first did prompt me to inquire;
He lent me counsel, and I lent him eyes.
I am no pilot; yet, wert thou as far
As that vast shore wash'd with the farthest sea,
I would adventure for such merchandise.

Suddenly embarrassed by the realization that Romeo has overheard her earlier claims of love for him, Juliet shyly remarks:

Thou know'st the mask of night is on my face,
Else would a maiden blush bepaint my cheek
For that which thou hast heard me speak to-night.
Fain would I dwell on form, fain, fain deny
What I have spoke: but farewell compliment!
Dost thou love me? I know thou wilt say 'Ay,'
And I will take thy word: yet, if thou swear'st,
Thou mayst prove false: at lovers' perjuries,
They say, Jove laughs. O gentle Romeo,
If thou dost love, pronounce it faithfully:
Or if thou think'st I am too quickly won,
I'll frown and be perverse and say thee nay,
So thou wilt woo; but else, not for the world.

In truth, fair Montague, I am too fond;
And therefore thou mayst think my 'haviour light:
But trust me, gentleman, I'll prove more true
Than those that have more cunning to be strange.
I should have been more strange, I must confess,
But that thou overheard'st, ere I was ware,
My true love's passion: therefore pardon me,
And not impute this yielding to light love,
Which the dark night hath so discovered.

Romeo starts to answer this apology by swearing "by yonder blessed moon" that he loves her. "O, swear not by the moon, th' inconstant moon/That monthly changes in her circled orb," begs Juliet. "Do not swear at all," she says, or "swear by thy gracious self . . . And I'll believe thee." Still cautious and uncertain, she continues:

Well, do not swear: although I joy in thee,
I have no joy of this contract to-night:
It is too rash, too unadvised, too sudden,
Too like the lightning, which doth cease to be
Ere one can say 'It lightens.' Sweet, good night!
This bud of love, by summer's ripening breath,
May prove a beauteous flower when next we meet.
Good night, good night! as sweet repose and rest
Come to thy heart as that within my breast!

Saying good night to Romeo, Juliet goes inside to answer the nurse's call. She returns shortly, however, and tells him:

Three words, dear Romeo, and good night indeed.
If that thy bent of love be honourable,
Thy purpose marriage, send me word to-morrow,
By one that I'll procure to come to thee,
Where and what time thou wilt perform the rite,
And all my fortunes at thy foot I'll lay,
And follow thee my lord throughout the world.

Again Juliet disappears, only to return momentarily to finalize the next day's plans. They agree that Juliet shall send a message to Romeo at nine o'clock the next morning. Finally, they say good night:

> **Juliet:** Good night, good night! parting is such sweet sorrow
> That I shall say good night till it be morrow.
> **Romeo:** Sleep dwell upon thine eyes, peace in thy breast!
> Would I were sleep and peace, so sweet to rest!
> Hence will I to my ghostly father's cell,
> His help to crave and my dear hap to tell.

In the early dawn, Friar Laurence appears with a basket:

> I must up-fill this osier cage of ours
> With baleful weeds and precious-juiced flowers.
> The earth that's nature's mother is her tomb;
> What is her burying grave, that is her womb:
> And from her womb children of divers kind
> We sucking on her natural bosom find,
> Many for many virtues excellent,
> None but for some, and yet all different.
> O, mickle is the powerful grace that lies
> In herbs, plants, stones, and their true qualities:
> For nought so vile that on the earth doth live,
> But to the earth some special good doth give;
> Nor aught so good, but, strain'd from that fair use,
> Revolts from true birth, stumbling on abuse:
> Virtue itself turns vice, being misapplied,
> And vice sometime's by action dignified.
> Within the infant rind of this small flower
> Poison hath residence, and medicine power:
> For this, being smelt, with that part cheers each part,
> Being tasted, slays all senses with the heart.
> Two such opposed kings encamp them still
> In man as well as herbs, grace and rude will;
> And where the worser is predominant,
> Full soon the canker death eats up that plant.

He is interrupted by Romeo, whom the friar accuses of having been up all night. When he pleads guilty, the Friar, who

16

is Romeo's confessor, asks if he has been with Rosaline, only to discover that Rosaline's place in Romeo's heart has been taken by another:

> **Romeo:** Then plainly know my heart's dear love is set
> On the fair daughter of rich Capulet:
> As mine on hers, so hers is set on mine;
> And all combined, save what thou must combine
> By holy marriage: when, and where, and how,
> We met, we woo'd and made exchange of vow,
> I'll tell thee as we pass; but this I pray,
> That thou consent to marry us to-day.

Surprised by this sudden change of affection, the friar comments on the fickleness of love:

> How much salt water thrown away in waste,
> To season love, that of it doth not taste!
> The sun not yet thy sighs from heaven clears,
> Thy old groans ring yet in mine ancient ears;
> Lo, here upon thy cheek the stain doth sit
> Of an old tear that is not wash'd off yet:
> If e'er thou wast thyself and these woes thine,
> Thou and these woes were all for Rosaline:
> And art thou changed? pronounce this sentence then:
> Women may fall when there's no strength in men.

Romeo has little patience for philosophy now. "I stand on haste," he tells the friar, who replies, "Wisely and slow; they stumble that run fast."

It is now fully morning, and Benvolio and Mercutio are still wondering where Romeo is. Tybalt has sent a letter to Montague that the two think to be a challenge. Mercutio says of him:

> O, he's the courageous captain of compliments. He
> fights as you sing prick-song, keeps time, distance and
> proportion; rests me his minim rest, one, two, and the
> third in your bosom: the very butcher of a silk button,
> a duellist, a duellist; a gentleman of the very first
> house, of the first and second cause.

17

At this moment, Romeo enters and is soon followed by the nurse and her man, Peter. She is looking for Romeo with a message from Juliet. Before she can deliver it, though, Mercutio steps in and begins to tease her. He confuses her by wishing her a good evening, although it is still noon. Then he makes a few typically indecent remarks, which the nurse responds to with pretended shock.

Left alone finally, the nurse and Romeo make arrangements for Juliet to slip away that afternoon to Friar Laurence's cell, where the young couple can be married. After giving the nurse a gift of money, which she pretends not to want but accepts, Romeo tells her that one of his men will bring a rope ladder to Juliet's window that night so that the newlywed couple can sleep together and consummate the marriage. The nurse continues to chatter about Paris' wish to marry Juliet and Juliet's association of Romeo with rosemary, the flower of remembrance used at weddings, but also at funerals.

Meanwhile, Juliet is impatiently awaiting the return of the nurse:

> The clock struck nine when I did send the nurse;
> In half an hour she promised to return.
> Perchance she cannot meet him: that's not so.
> O, she is lame! love's heralds should be thoughts,
> Which ten times faster glide than the sun's beams,
> Driving back shadows over louring hills:
> Therefore do nimble-pinion'd doves draw love,
> And therefore hath the wind-swift Cupid wings.
> Now is the sun upon the highmost hill
> Of this day's journey, and from nine till twelve
> Is three long hours; yet she is not come.
> Had she affections and warm youthful blood,
> She would be as swift in motion as a ball;
> My words would bandy her to my sweet love,
> And his to me:
> But old folks, many feign as they were dead;
> Unwieldy, slow, heavy and pale as lead.

The nurse finally arrives and is greeted anxiously by Juliet. After much stalling and teasing, the nurse finally answers Juliet's nervous questions:

Then hie you hence to Friar Laurence' cell;
There stays a husband to make you a wife:
Now comes the wanton blood up in your cheeks,
They'll be in scarlet straight at any news.
Hie you to church; I must another way,
To fetch a ladder, by the which your love
Must climb a bird's nest soon when it is dark;
I am the drudge, and toil in your delight;
But you shall bear the burthen soon at night.
Go; I'll to dinner; hie you to the cell.

That afternoon, at Friar Laurence's cell, Romeo and the friar are talking. The friar is advising moderation:

These violent delights have violent ends,
And in their triumph die; like fire and powder
Which as they kiss consume: the sweetest honey
Is loathsome in his own deliciousness,
And in the taste confounds the appetite:
Therefore, love moderately; long love doth so;
Too swift arrives as tardy as too slow.
                                    [*Enter Juliet*]

Here comes the lady. O, so light a foot
Will ne'er wear out the everlasting flint.
A lover may bestride the gossamer
That idles in the wanton summer air,
And yet not fall; so light is vanity.

The lovers greet each other in emotional, poetic language, and the friar comically puts an end to the scene by declaring that he must marry them before he will allow them to stay alone together.

ACT III

In a public place in Verona, Mercutio and Benvolio are talking. Because the day is hot and Capulets are walking about, Benvolio thinks they had better go inside. Mercutio thinks Benvolio cannot really mean that. He pretends to believe Benvolio is not the kind of man who would avoid a fight:

> Thou! why, thou wilt quarrel with a man that hath a hair more, or a hair less, in his beard than thou hast: thou wilt quarrel with a man for cracking nuts, having no other reason but because thou hast hazel eyes; what eye, but such an eye, would spy out such a quarrel? thy head is as full of quarrels as an egg is full of meat, and yet thy head hath been beaten as addle as an egg for quarrelling: thou hast quarrelled with a man for coughing in the street, because he hath wakened thy dog that hath lain asleep in the sun: didst thou not fall out with a tailor for wearing his new doublet before Easter? with another, for tying his new shoes with old riband? and yet thou wilt tutor me from quarrelling!
>
> **Benvolio:** An I were so apt to quarrel as thou art, any man should buy the fee-simple of my life for an hour and a quarter.

Just then, the Capulets appear, led by Tybalt. He is hunting for Romeo, but is willing to take on any Montague. Benvolio tries to keep Mercutio and Tybalt from quarrelling, and is successful only because Tybalt sees Romeo and turns to challenge him. Romeo refuses to fight, saying that he now has reason to love Tybalt. Tybalt continues to insult Romeo, whose mild response seems, to Mercutio, to be a sign of "calm, dishonourable, vile submission."

Mercutio and Tybalt draw their swords and begin to fight. Romeo steps between them, and Tybalt takes the opportunity to thrust his sword under Romeo's arm and into Mercutio's side. Tybalt runs, and Mercutio cries:

> I am hurt;
> A plague o' both your houses! I am sped:
> Is he gone, and hath nothing?

Mercutio assures his friends that his wound is just "a scratch." He adds:

> No, 'tis not so deep as a well, nor so wide as a church-door; but 'tis enough, 'twill serve: ask for me to-morrow, and you shall find me a grave man. I am peppered, I warrant, for this world. A plague o' both your houses! 'Zounds, a dog, a rat, a mouse, a cat, to scratch a man to death! a braggart, a rogue, a villain, that fights by the book of arithmetic! Why the devil came you between us? I was hurt under your arm.

The dying man asks Benvolio to help him inside.
Realizing that Mercutio's wound is fatal, Romeo exclaims:

> O sweet Juliet,
> Thy beauty hath made me effeminate,
> And in my temper soften'd valour's steel!

When Benvolio re-enters to announce Mercutio's death, Romeo swears that he will have revenge on Tybalt.

Tybalt returns and begins to scorn Romeo by calling him a "wretched boy." In the fight that follows, Romeo kills Tybalt. Benvolio urges Romeo to run, or else "the prince will doom thee death/If thou art taken." "O, I am fortune's fool!" cries Romeo.

As Romeo flees, citizens enter, followed by the prince, Montague, Capulet and their wives. Benvolio gives the prince an account of this latest fight. When he has heard the story, the prince pronounces judgment on Romeo:

> And for that offence
> Immediately we do exile him hence:
> I have an interest in your hate's proceeding,
> My blood for your rude brawls doth lie a-bleeding;
> But I'll amerce you with so strong a fine,
> That you shall all repent the loss of mine:
> I will be deaf to pleading and excuses;
> Nor tears nor prayers shall purchase out abuses:
> Therefore use none: let Romeo hence in haste,
> Else, when he's found, that hour is his last.

Bear hence this body, and attend our will:
Mercy but murders, pardoning those that kill.

Meanwhile, Juliet, who knows nothing of what has happened, waits for night to fall and Romeo to come to her:

Gallop apace, you fiery-footed steeds,
Towards Phœbus' lodging: such a waggoner
As Phaethon would whip you to the west,
And bring in cloudy night immediately.
Spread thy close curtain, love-performing night,
That runaways' eyes may wink, and Romeo
Leap to these arms, untalk'd of and unseen.
Lovers can see to do their amorous rites
By their own beauties; or, if love be blind,
It best agrees with night. Come, civil night,
Thou sober-suited matron, all in black,
And learn me how to lose a winning match,
Play'd for a pair of stainless maidenhoods:
Hood my unmann'd blood bating in my cheeks
With thy black mantle, till strange love grown bold
Think true love acted simple modesty.
Come, night, come, Romeo, come, thou day in night;
For thou wilt lie upon the wings of night
Whiter than new snow on a raven's back.
Come, gentle night, come, loving, black-brow'd night,
Give me my Romeo; and, when he shall die,
Take him and cut him out in little stars,
And he will make the face of heaven so fine,
That all the world will be in love with night,
And pay no worship to the garish sun.
O, I have bought the mansion of a love,
But not possess'd it, and, though I am sold,
Not yet enjoy'd; so tedious is this day
As is the night before some festival
To an impatient child that hath new robes
And may not wear them. O, here comes my nurse,
And she brings news, and every tongue that speaks
But Romeo's name speaks heavenly eloquence.
Now, nurse, what news? What hast thou there? the
cords
That Romeo bid thee fetch?

Suddenly, the nurse begins wailing over someone who is dead, repeating the name of Romeo. Juliet concludes that Romeo has been killed, but the nurse begins to mourn over Tybalt. Juliet is greatly confused until the nurse says that Romeo has killed Tybalt and is banished. Juliet exclaims against Romeo:

> O serpent heart, hid with a flowering face!
> Did ever dragon keep so fair a cave?
> Beautiful tyrant! fiend angelical!
> Dove-feather'd raven! wolvish-ravening lamb!
> Despised substance of divinest show!
> Just opposite to what thou justly seem'st,
> A damned saint, and honourable villain!
> O nature, what hadst thou to do in hell,
> When thou didst bower the spirit of a fiend
> In mortal paradise of such sweet flesh?
> Was ever book containing such vile matter
> So fairly bound? O, that deceit should dwell
> In such a gorgeous palace!

But she regrets this outburst almost immediately.
Soon she remembers that she has heard the word "banished" and begins to talk about it:

> 'Romeo is banished:' to speak that word,
> Is father, mother, Tybalt, Romeo, Juliet,
> All slain, all dead. 'Romeo is banished.'
> There is no end, no limit, measure, bound,
> In that word's death; no words can that woe sound.

At last, however, the nurse gives Juliet the news that Romeo will be with her that night. Then, the lovers can say their last farewell.

Meanwhile, Romeo has taken refuge at Friar Laurence's cell. Romeo, too, is overwhelmed by the thought that he is banished:

> 'Tis torture, and not mercy: heaven is here,
> Where Juliet lives; and every cat and dog
> And little mouse, every unworthy thing,

Live here in heaven and may look on her,
But Romeo may not: more validity,
More honourable state, more courtship lives
In carrion-flies than Romeo: they may seize
On the white wonder of dear Juliet's hand,
And steal immortal blessing from her lips;
Who, even in pure and vestal modesty,
Still blush, as thinking their own kisses sin;
But Romeo may not; he is banished:
This may flies do, but I from this must fly:
They are free men, but I am banished:
And say'st thou yet, that exile is not death?
Hadst thou no poison mix'd, no sharp-ground knife,
No sudden mean of death, though ne'er so mean,
But 'banished' to kill me?—'Banished'?
O friar, the damned use that word in hell;
Howling attends it: how hast thou the heart,
Being a divine, a ghostly confessor,
A sin-absolver, and my friend profess'd,
To mangle me with that word 'banished'?

As Romeo throws himself upon the ground in his grief, the
nurse comes to tell them of Juliet's mourning over Tybalt and
Romeo. This leads Romeo to draw his sword to kill himself. The
friar stops him with determined and angry speech and goes on to
tell him of his good fortune in escaping the death Tybalt had in
mind for him.

Friar Laurence then suggests that Romeo go to Juliet and
comfort her. But the friar warns him to leave before morning
and escape to Mantua, where he must hide until the friar makes
a return possible:

To blaze your marriage, reconcile your friends,
Beg pardon of the prince, and call thee back
With twenty hundred thousand times more joy
Than thou went'st forth in lamentation.

The friar promises to send Romeo, in Mantua, news of
affairs in Verona by his man. Thus the friar plans for the lovers
as best he can.

The Capulets are also planning. Old Capulet apologizes to

Paris because he has had no chance to speak to Juliet about the marriage. Paris agrees with Capulet that these are no times to woo. Capulet promises Paris that he will talk to Juliet at once. He is so sure she will do what he wishes that he even sets the wedding for the following Thursday, this being Monday. He then sends Lady Capulet to prepare her daughter "against this wedding day."

It is now morning, and Romeo and Juliet must say good-bye. She speaks:

Wilt thou be gone? it is not yet near day:
It was the nightingale, and not the lark,
That pierced the fearful hollow of thine ear;
Nightly she sings on yond pomegranate-tree:
Believe me, love, it was the nightingale.
Romeo: It was the lark, the herald of the morn,
No nightingale: look, love, what envious streaks
Do lace the severing clouds in yonder east:
Night's candles are burnt out, and jocund day
Stands tiptoe on the misty mountain tops:
I must be gone and live, or stay and die.
Juliet: Yond light is not day-light, I know it, I:
It is some meteor that the sun exhales,
To be to thee this night a torch-bearer,
And light thee on thy way to Mantua:
Therefore stay yet; thou need'st not to be gone.
Romeo: Let me be ta'en, let me be put to death;
I am content, so thou wilt have it so.
I'll say yon grey is not the morning's eye,
'Tis but the pale reflex of Cynthia's brow;
Nor that is not the lark, whose notes do beat
The vaulty heaven so high above our heads:
I have more care to stay than will to go:
Come, death, and welcome! Juliet wills it so.
How is 't my soul? let's talk: it is not day.
Juliet: It is, it is: hie hence, be gone, away!
It is the lark that sings so out of tune,
Straining harsh discords and unpleasing sharps.
Some say the lark makes sweet division;
This doth not so, for she divideth us:
Some say the lark and loathed toad change eyes;

O, now I would they had changed voices too!
Since arm from arm that voice doth us affray,
Hunting thee hence with hunts-up to the day.
O, now be gone; more light and light it grows.
Romeo: More light and light: more dark and dark our
woes!

The nurse enters to warn them that Juliet's mother is
coming, and Romeo descends the rope ladder. As Juliet looks
down at him from her window, she says:

O God! I have an ill-divining soul.
Methinks I see thee, now thou art below,
As one dead in the bottom of a tomb:
Either my eyesight fails or thou look'st pale.

Lady Capulet, coming into the room, finds Juliet crying
and thinks it is for Tybalt. Lady Capulet offers to send someone
to Mantua to poison Romeo, to which Juliet replies in a speech
with double meaning:

Madam if you could find out but a man
To bear a poison, I would temper it,
That Romeo should, upon receipt thereof,
Soon sleep in quiet. O, how my heart abhors
To hear him named, and cannot come to him,
To wreak the love I bore my cousin
Upon his body that hath slaughter'd him!

Lady Capulet now tells her daughter the news that Juliet's
father has chosen a husband, Paris, for Juliet, to whom she is to
be married on Thursday. Juliet, of course, refuses to agree to
this. Rather Romeo than Paris, she exclaims. At this moment,
her father comes in to find his daughter in tears and Lady
Capulet angry because Juliet refuses to do as her father desires.
He cannot understand this disrespect:

God's bread! it makes me mad:
Day, night, hour, tide, time, work, play,
Alone, in company, still my care hath been
To have her match'd: and having now provided

A gentleman of noble parentage,
Of fair demesnes, youthful, and nobly train'd,
Stuff'd, as they say, with honourable parts,
Proportion'd as one's thought would wish a man;
And then to have a wretched puling fool,
A whining mammet, in her fortune's tender,
To answer 'I'll not wed; I cannot love,
I am too young; I pray you, pardon me.'
But, an you will not wed, I'll pardon you:
Graze where you will, you shall not house with me:
Look to 't, think on 't, I do not use to jest.
Thursday is near; lay hand on heart, advise:
An you be mine, I'll give you to my friend;
An you be not, hang, beg, starve, die in the streets,
For, by my soul, I'll ne'er acknowledge thee,
Nor what is mine shall never do thee good:
Trust to 't, bethink you; I'll not be forsworn.

After he has gone, Juliet appeals to her mother: "Is there no pity sitting in the clouds/That sees into the bottom of my grief?" But her mother also turns against her, and even the nurse, who alone knows the whole story, is unsympathetic. To Juliet's plea for comfort, the nurse replies:

Faith, here it is.
Romeo is banish'd, and all the world to nothing,
That he dares ne'er come back to challenge you;
Of, if he do, it needs must be by stealth.
Then, since the case so stands as now it doth,
I think it best you married with the county.
O, he's a lovely gentleman!
Romeo's a dishclout to him: an eagle, madam,
Hath not so green, so quick, so fair an eye
As Paris hath.

Remembering how the nurse had praised Romeo before, Juliet wonders how she can be so hypocritical now. After dismissing the nurse, Juliet says:

Thou and my bosom henceforth shall be twain.
I'll to the friar, to know his remedy:
If all else fail, myself have power to die.

ACT IV

When Juliet reaches Friar Laurence's cell, she finds Paris there, arranging for the friar to perform the marriage ceremony. Paris greets her warmly: "Happily met, my lady and my wife!" But Juliet manages to avoid Paris' attempt to woo her. When he is gone, she turns to Friar Laurence and declares that she is "past hope, past cure, past help!" If the friar cannot give her advice, she will kill herself. Friar Laurence offers her "a kind of hope," but she must have "strength of will" to "undertake/A thing like death." He outlines his plan:

> Hold, then; go home, be merry, give consent
> To marry Paris: Wednesday is to-morrow;
> To-morrow night look that thou lie alone,
> Let not thy nurse lie with thee in thy chamber:
> Take thou this vial, being then in bed,
> And this distilled liquor drink thou off:
> When presently through all thy veins shall run
> A cold and drowsy humour; for no pulse
> Shall keep his native progress, but surcease:
> No warmth, no breath, shall testify thou livest;
> The roses in thy lips and cheeks shall fade
> To paly ashes; thy eyes' windows fall,
> Like death, when he shuts up the day of life;
> Each part, deprived of supple government,
> Shall, stiff and stark and cold, appear like death:
> And in this borrow'd likeness of shrunk death
> Thou shalt continue two and forty hours,
> And then awake as from a pleasant sleep.
> Now, when the bridegroom in the morning comes
> To rouse thee from thy bed, there art thou dead:
> Then, as the manner of our country is,
> In thy best robes uncover'd on the bier
> Thou shalt be borne to that same ancient vault
> Where all the kindred of the Capulets lie.
> In the mean time, against thou shalt awake,
> Shall Romeo by my letters know our drift;
> And hither shall he come: and he and I
> Will watch thy waking, and that very night
> Shall Romeo bear thee hence to Mantua.
> And this shall free thee from this present shame,

If no inconstant toy nor womanish fear
Abate thy valour in the acting it.

Juliet calls on "Love" to give her strength and hurries off.

Juliet returns to her home and tells her father that the friar has persuaded her to go through with the wedding. In his joy over this, her father says they will not wait until Thursday, but will have the wedding the next morning. Juliet and the nurse begin to make the necessary preparations. When these are completed, Juliet dismisses the nurse. When her mother comes in, she tells her everything is arranged and that she wishes to be alone. Lady Capulet leaves, and Juliet is left with her thoughts:

Farewell! God knows when we shall meet again.
I have a faint cold fear thrills through my veins,
That almost freezes up the heat of life:
I'll call them back again to comfort me.
Nurse!—What should she do here?
My dismal scene I needs must act alone.
Come, vial.
What if this mixture do not work at all?
Shall I be married then to-morrow morning?
No, no: this shall forbid it. Lie thou there.
                    [Laying down a dagger]
What if it be a poison, which the friar
Subtly hath minister'd to have me dead,
Lest in this marriage he should be dishonour'd,
Because he married me before to Romeo?
I fear it is: and yet, methinks, it should not,
For he hath still been tried a holy man.
How if, when I am laid into the tomb,
I wake before the time that Romeo
Come to redeem me? there's a fearful point.
Shall I not then be stifled in the vault,
To whose foul mouth no healthsome air breathes in,
And there die strangled ere my Romeo comes?
Or, if I live, is it not very like,
The horrible conceit of death and night,
Together with the terror of the place,
As in a vault, an ancient receptacle,
Where for this many hundred years the bones

Of all my buried ancestors are pack'd;
Where bloody Tybalt, yet but green in earth,
Lies festering in his shroud; where, as they say,
At some hours in the night spirits resort;
Alack, alack, is it not like that I
So early waking, what with loathsome smells
And shrieks like mandrakes' torn out of the earth,
That living mortals hearing them run mad:
O, if I wake, shall I not be distraught,
Environed with all these hideous fears?
And madly play with my forefathers' joints?
And pluck the mangled Tybalt from his shroud?
And, in this rage, with some great kinsman's bone,
As with a club, dash out my desperate brains?
O, look! methinks I see my cousin's ghost
Seeking out Romeo, that did spit his body
Upon a rapier's point: stay, Tybalt, stay!
Romeo, I come! this do I drink to thee.

Early on the morning of Juliet's wedding day, the nurse is
sent to waken Juliet and is astonished to find her mistress
dressed and lying on her bed, apparently dead. She calls her
parents, who are overcome with grief. Friar Laurence arrives
with Paris, and the sad news is revealed. It is only by the most
strenuous effort that Friar Laurence can calm everyone down
enough to make arrangements for the funeral. The general
feeling is expressed by Juliet's father:

All things that we ordained festival,
Turn from their office to black funeral:
Our instruments to melancholy bells;
Our wedding cheer to a sad burial feast;
Our solemn hymns to sullen dirges change;
Our bridal flowers serve for a buried corse,
And all things change them to the contrary.

ACT V

In Mantua, Romeo has just awakened from a pleasant dream:

> If I may trust the flattering truth of sleep,
> My dreams presage some joyful news at hand:
> My bosom's lord sits lightly in his throne,
> And all this day an unaccustom'd spirit
> Lifts me above the ground with cheerful thoughts.
> I dreamt my lady came and found me dead—
> Strange dream, that gives a dead man leave to think!—
> And breathed such life with kisses in my lips,
> That I revived and was an emperor.
> Ah me! how sweet is love itself possess'd,
> When but love's shadows are so rich in joy!

Balthasar enters. When Romeo asks about Juliet, he answers that she is well because "Her body sleeps in Capel's monument, / And her immortal part with angels lives." Romeo's response is simple and direct in its sorrow: "Is it even so? Then I defy you, stars!" Romeo prepares to leave for Verona that night, although Balthasar urges him to have patience. Romeo asks whether there are any letters from Friar Laurence and, learning that there are none, dismisses Balthasar and quickly plans what action he must take:

> Well, Juliet, I will lie with thee to-night.
> Let's see for means: O mischief, thou art swift
> To enter in the thoughts of desperate men!

He then remembers a druggist nearby, whose poverty would make him desperate enough to sell poison, even though the law forbids such a sale. Romeo persuades the man to take 40 gold coins in exchange for "a dram of poison, such soon-speeding gear / As will disperse itself through all the veins."

At the same time, Friar Laurence is learning from Friar John, a brother of his order, whom he had sent with an explanatory letter to Romeo, that, because of a quarantine into which he had stumbled while seeking a brother to go with him to Mantua, he had not been able to get to Mantua at all. Friar Laurence immediately decides to go to the monument alone and, meanwhile, to send another letter to Romeo. He plans to keep the awakened Juliet at his cell until Romeo returns.

That night, Paris goes to the tomb of Juliet, bearing flowers. He orders his page to listen for any approaching footsteps and, if he hears anyone, to whistle. Standing in front of the tomb, Paris speaks:

> Sweet flower, with flowers thy bridal bed I strew,
>   O woe! thy canopy is dust and stones;
> Which with sweet water nightly I will dew,
>   Or, wanting that, with tears distill'd by moans:
> The obsequies that I for thee will keep
> Nightly shall be to strew thy grave and weep.

He is interrupted by the page's whistle and steps to one side as Romeo and Balthasar appear with a torch, crowbar and other tools. Romeo takes the tools from Balthasar and gives his servant a letter to his parents, explaining the reason for his death. Telling Balthasar that he is entering the tomb to see Juliet's face and to take a ring from her finger, Romeo sends his servant away, warning him not to return. But Balthasar, suspecting that his master has lied to him, decides:

> [*Aside*] For all this same, I'll hide me hereabout:
> His looks I fear, and his intents I doubt.   [*Retires*]

Romeo, supposing that he has been left alone, now addresses the tomb:

> Thou detestable maw, thou womb of death,
> Gorged with the dearest morsel of the earth,
> Thus I enforce thy rotten jaws to open,
> And in despite I'll cram thee with more food.
>   [*Opens the tomb*]

But, before Romeo can enter the tomb, Paris steps forward and challenges him. Romeo begs Paris not to "tempt a desperate man;/Fly hence and leave me." But Paris refuses to leave and he is killed in the fight that follows. As he dies, Paris asks to be placed in the tomb with Juliet. Romeo, recognizing Paris as a

Capulet and recalling that he was to be married to Juliet, sympathizes with the dead youth:

> O, give me thy hand,
> One writ with me in sour misfortune's book!
> I'll bury thee in a triumphant grave;
> A grave? O, no, a lantern, slaughter'd youth;
> For here lies Juliet, and her beauty makes
> This vault a feasting presence full of light.
> Death, lie thou there, by a dead man interr'd.
>   [*Laying Paris in the monument*]
> How oft when men are at the point of death
> Have they been merry! which their keepers call
> A lightning before death: O, how may I
> Call this a lightning? O my love! my wife!
> Death, that hath suck'd the honey of thy breath,
> Hath had no power yet upon thy beauty:
> Thou art not conquer'd; beauty's ensign yet
> Is crimson in thy lips and in thy cheeks,
> And death's pale flag is not advanced there.
> Tybalt, liest thou there in thy bloody sheet?
> O, what more favour can I do to thee
> Than with that hand that cut thy youth in twain
> To sunder his that was thine enemy?
> Forgive me, cousin! Ah, dear Juliet,
> Why art thou yet so fair? shall I believe
> That unsubstantial death is amorous,
> And that the lean abhorred monster keeps
> Thee here in dark to be his paramour?
> For fear of that, I still will stay with thee,
> And never from this palace of dim night
> Depart again: here, here will I remain
> With worms that are thy chamber-maids; O, here
> Will I set up my everlasting rest,
> And shake the yoke of inauspicious stars
> From this world-wearied flesh. Eyes, look your last!
> Arms, take your last embrace! and, lips, O you
> The doors of breath, seal with a righteous kiss
> A dateless bargain to engrossing death!
> Come, bitter conduct, come, unsavoury guide!
> Thou desperate pilot, now at once run on

The dashing rocks thy sea-sick weary bark.
Here's to my love! [*Drinks*] O true apothecary!
Thy drugs are quick. Thus with a kiss I die.

Then, Friar Laurence enters the churchyard, with a lantern,
crowbar and spade, and meets Balthasar, who tells him that
Romeo has been in the tomb for half an hour. The friar goes
fearfully toward it, calling to Romeo. When he enters, he finds
Juliet just awakening from her sleep. When she asks for Romeo,
Friar Laurence tells her what has happened and says he will hide
her in a sisterhood of nuns. Juliet refuses to go with him. Alone
in the tomb, Juliet attempts to kill herself:

What's here? A cup, closed in my true love's hand?
Poison, I see, hath been his timeless end:
O churl! drunk all, and left no friendly drop
To help me after? I will kiss thy lips;
Haply some poison yet doth hang on them,
To make me die with a restorative.   [*Kisses him*]
Thy lips are warm.

Hearing the voice of a watchman approaching, Juliet
desperately takes Romeo's dagger and stabs herself. She falls on
his body and dies.

The watchman, called by Paris' page, now comes and
discovers the dead bodies. They bring in Balthasar and the friar,
just as the prince enters, followed by Capulet and his lady. The
guards explain what they have found in the tomb. As they are
mourning, Montague, whose wife has died over grief for
Romeo, joins them. Then the friar tells his story. Balthasar
enters and hands the prince a letter given him by Romeo addressed to Montague. The prince reads it, and says it confirms
what the others have told. "See, what a scourge is laid upon
your hate," the prince sadly observes to Capulet and Montague.

The families agree that heaven has found "means to kill
[their] joys with love." A reconciliation follows:

Capulet: O brother Montague, give me thy hand:
This is my daughter's jointure, for no more
Can I demand.
Montague: But I can give thee more:

For I will raise her statue in pure gold;
That whiles Verona by that name is known,
There shall no figure at such rate be set
As that of true and faithful Juliet.
Capulet: As rich shall Romeo's by his lady's lie;
Poor sacrifices of our enmity!

The prince sums up the tragedy of these two lovers:

A glooming peace this morning with it brings;
    The sun for sorrow will not show his head:
Go hence, to have more talk of these sad things;
    Some shall be pardon'd and some punished:
For never was a story of more woe
Than this of Juliet and her Romeo.

Part B: Questions and Answers by Act and Scene
ACT I · PROLOGUE
Question 1.
Explain the terms, "prologue" and "chorus." What purpose do they serve? Which other plays by Shakespeare have a chorus?

Answer

"Prologue" is the name given to introductory verses spoken before a dramatic performance or play begins. Sometimes the word is used to describe the speaker of these verses. More often, however, the prologue is spoken by the chorus.

The term, "chorus," refers to a tradition that comes from Greek tragedy and was commonly used in early English drama to interpret events about to happen on the stage, or to explain what has happened in the intervals between the acts.

In Shakespeare's time, the sounding of trumpets used to announce to the audience that the play was about to begin. At the third sounding, the prologue, or chorus, entered, always dressed in black and wearing an expression of humility. He would then explain the action of the play and possibly provide the intended moral. Even before Shakespeare began to write, however, the presence of a chorus was becoming old-fashioned. He uses it only in this play (in which it is dropped after the second act), *The Winter's Tale, Henry VIII* and *Henry V*.

Question 2.
The chorus is omitted in the first collected edition of Shakespeare's plays and in later acting editions. Suggest reasons for this omission.

Answer

When viewing a play, we should have our curiosity aroused, so that we experience fears, doubts and hopes, and have our uncertainties and expectations kept alive until the end. Therefore, putting ourselves in the position of spectators of this play, we would prefer not to know from the beginning that both the lovers are to die at the end. Moreover, the action of the play needs no explaining. The first scene plunges us at once into the middle of the feud between the two houses, and both the hero and the heroine are introduced to us in the first act. It probably was for these reasons that the prologue was cut out. It unnecessarily lengthened a play that was already long enough.

ACT I · SCENE 1

Question 1.
Comment on the order in which the characters appear in the first scene.

Answer
Note the balanced grouping of the characters. Two Capulet servants are followed by two Montague servants. Then, the peace-loving Benvolio of the Montague side is followed by the quarrelsome Tybalt of the Capulet side. Then, citizens of both sides enter, followed by the appearance of Capulet and Lady Capulet, followed by Montague and Lady Montague. The neutral prince follows, "as keystone to bind all together," and, finally, at some distance, the hero of the play, who would be neutral if he could, but whom circumstances force to be the most active element of the feud, arrives.

Question 2.
Is there any distinction between Sampson and Gregory?

Answer
Sampson is a boaster and has the weaker intellect. Gregory has more intellect and makes fun of Sampson. When the time comes for action, Sampson hides behind the law. Gregory, who has a "swashing blow," is the more powerful of the two.

Question 3.
Contrast the behavior of Benvolio and Tybalt, showing how each displays an important characteristic.

Answer
Benvolio is a lover of peace and separates the fighters, while Tybalt is hot-tempered, hates the word "peace" and adds fuel to the smouldering fire.

Question 4.
Describe Romeo's first appearance in the scene. How does he speak of love?

Answer
When Romeo appears, he is moody, unaware of the passage of time, indifferent to what has occurred and, generally, "lost to the world." When he speaks of love, it is in abstract terms, or in phrases that he might have read in a book. He indulges in word play with Benvolio. In love with love, he seems to speak from his mind only, not from his heart. He also generalizes. He states that love is blind, that her "view is muffled still" and that he is not himself when he is in love. Later, we shall see how differently he expresses himself when he is really in love.

Question 5.
Why does the play open with a street quarrel between servants?

Answer
The development of the play is based on the quarrel between the Capulets and Montagues, and the street fight makes that announcement to the audience. It begins with servants to show that the feud extends to all the members of the families. The heads of the houses do not at any time quarrel directly with each other, in obedience to the commands of the prince. Sampson and Gregory know that they are not supposed to argue publicly and plan not to be held responsible for beginning a fight, but they are eager enough to participate in one. The heads of the houses and the prince enter shortly to explain conditions leading to the fight.

ACT I · SCENE 2
Question 1.
What probably has happened between Scenes 1 and 2?

Answer
The first line of this scene shows us that the prince has acquainted Montague and Capulet with his "further pleasure,"

referred to in Scene 1, and that the heads of both families have been ordered to keep the peace.

Question 2.
What impression of Capulet do you receive from this scene?

Answer
He appears here as the loving father, reluctant to exercise his parental authority, kind and hospitable, and wishing to please Paris, the kinsman to the prince. We shall find later that there is another side to Capulet's character.

Question 3.
How does Capulet's letter of invitation further the plot?

Answer
The fact that the servant cannot read the list of names leads to the encounter with Romeo and Benvolio. When he reads the list for the servant, Romeo learns that Rosaline is invited to the feast and he follows Benvolio's suggestion to attend. Because the guests at the party will be masked, Romeo will not be recognized as a Montague.

ACT I · SCENE 3

Question 1.
What purposes do the nurse's speeches serve?

Answer
They establish her as a talkative, crude and lively character, just the type to enter eagerly into the secret courtship of Romeo and Juliet. Her words also emphasize Juliet's youth, natural innocence and dignity.

Question 2.
Compare Lady Capulet's and the nurse's words about Paris.

Answer
Lady Capulet, in an elaborate metaphor, compares Paris to a book. Delight is "writ" in his face with beauty's pen, she says,

and what is hidden in his face is written in the margin of his eyes. Lady Capulet ends her long praise with the words, "So shall you share all that he doth possess,/By having him making yourself no less." The nurse immediately protests: "No less! Nay bigger! Women grow by men." The nurse's coarse, blunt statement contrasts sharply with the delicate thoughts and artificial wording of Lady Capulet's speech. The nurse deflates the pretty sentiments of Lady Capulet's speech and abruptly reminds us of the physical side of marriage.

ACT I · SCENE 4

Question 1.
Are the jokes and mocking speeches in this scene appropriate in a tragedy?

Answer
The play would be dull if it contained nothing but love scenes and gloomy tragedy. The mockery in this scene, then, adds variety to the play.

The witty remarks of Mercutio are, as we shall realize later, consistent with his character. He is the Elizabethan aristocrat, lively, brilliant, light-hearted—a complete contrast to the reserved Romeo. The punning and exchange of wit in this scene would have seemed quite natural to an Elizabethan audience, for such contests of wit were a favorite pastime of the cultured aristocrats of the day.

That Romeo also should join in this battle of wits requires no further explanation than his own: "Misery makes sport to mock itself."

Question 2.
Discuss the relevance of Mercutio's Queen Mab speech.

Answer
Mercutio is:

One whom the music of his own vain tongue
Doth ravish like enchanting harmony

and, therefore, any poetic speech is in harmony with his character, but the speech is not dramatically necessary. It is an ornament only. It does not further the action of the play, nor does it help us to understand Mercutio's character. Shakespeare probably could not resist the temptation to write beautiful poetry for its own sake. This is a mark of the dramatist's early period of composition.

ACT I · SCENE 5

Question 1.

Why is the first part of the scene—the preparations of the servants—included?

Answer

It gives the impression of confused preparation and bustle, forming a contrast to the more dignified, solemn atmosphere that ends the act. There is a slight feeling of suspense during the delay, as the audience waits for the arrival of Romeo and his friends. The humor of the servants' preparations also interrupts the progress of the tragedy and lowers the level of action so that the next important development in the plot seems more effective by contrast.

Question 2.

Comment on the poetry of Romeo's and Juliet's first words to each other.

Answer

Their first words to each other form a sonnet. Romeo speaks the first quatrain, Juliet the second and they share the third. Each one speaks a line of the closing couplet. They immediately begin another sonnet. Each, in turn, speaks a line of the first quatrain until the fourth line, which is divided between them.

The use of the sonnet form heightens the intensity of the romance that springs up so suddenly between Romeo and Juliet. The tenderness and sacredness of their love is emphasized in their poetry.

ACT II · PROLOGUE

Question 1.

What is the purpose of the prologue to Act II?

Answer

The prologue adds little to the progress of the plot, but it does review what is already known and it hints at what will happen in the next scene. The prologue may have been included to pass time while the stage was being changed.

ACT II · SCENE 1

Question 1.

Describe the attitude of Mercutio and Benvolio toward Romeo's love.

Answer

Benvolio feels a certain sympathy with Romeo, although he thinks the latter's love to be mere infatuation. To Mercutio, "madman" and "lover" are all one. He is Romeo's friend and wishes to cure him of a disease, he himself knowing no love that is not purely physical. Romeo, from within the wall, expresses Mercutio's attitude in the words: "He jests at scars that never felt a wound."

ACT II · SCENE 2

Question 1.

In what kind of speeches do Romeo and Juliet respectively express their feelings?

Answer

Romeo's language is more imaginative, containing many similes, metaphors and images introduced for decoration only. Juliet's language is as poetic in thought and substance as Romeo's, but she expresses herself more simply.

Question 2.

What characteristics of Romeo and Juliet may be clearly seen through their speeches?

Answer

Romeo is the idealist, Juliet the realist. Romeo is romantic; Juliet is more matter-of-fact. She asks clear and definite questions, while his replies are vague and full of airy notions. She, being practical, has to make plans; he lives for the moment and for her alone. The instant she leaves, he fears "all this is but a dream." He is drunk with love and will sacrifice name, family, everything, if only she may belong to him.

Question 3.
How does this scene advance or change the progress of the action?

Answer
This scene gives us a clearer knowledge of the depth of the passionate love of the hero and heroine and some further insight into their characters, particularly Juliet's, about which we know little. The fact that Romeo overhears Juliet expressing her love for him makes it possible for them to proceed quickly with their plans. If he had not discovered her true feelings so soon, a long courtship might have taken place, which would have had entirely different consequences from the hasty and secret marriage.

ACT II · SCENE 3

Question 1.
How does Friar Laurence's soliloquy represent a major theme of the play?

Answer
His soliloquy is filled with figures of speech illustrating the opposite qualities of herbs; good and evil are contrasted. The friar's words can be regarded as a comment on the play itself:

> For nought so vile that on the earth doth live,
> But to the earth some special good doth give; . . .
> Virtue itself turns vice, being misapplied,
> And vice sometime's by action dignified.

Thus, the unfortunate tragedy of the lovers' deaths has a good result in finally uniting the feuding families in a common loss.

Question 2.
Why is the friar so easily persuaded to help with the secret marriage?

Answer

His ignorance of the world, his own pureness of heart, his belief in moderation, together with his affection for the lovers, whose union he thinks will be a holy act, and his imagined skill in dealing with human actions, all combine to cause him to welcome this opportunity of healing (as he expects) the conflict between the rival houses.

ACT II · SCENE 4

Question 1.

What indications are there in this scene of what Romeo was like before falling in love with Rosaline?

Answer

After the exchange of wit between himself and Romeo, Mercutio says: "Now art thou sociable, now art thou Romeo; now art thou what thou art, by art as well as by nature," from which we may conclude that Romeo was formerly carefree and high-spirited. He appears to have been more sympathetic toward Benvolio than toward Mercutio.

Question 2.

Why does the nurse seek out Romeo, and how does she go about her errand?

Answer

The nurse says that she desires "confidence" with Romeo and that her young lady "bade me inquire you out." She goes about her work, as one might expect, in the most roundabout way possible. She has been present on the stage for 17 lines before Romeo knows that she has come from Juliet. Even then, his knowledge is intelligent guesswork.

Question 3.

What new characteristics of the nurse are apparent in this scene?

Answer

We have already had proof that she is talkative and ignorant. We have also seen that she has loved Juliet (in her own way) from a baby. We now learn, from her behavior with the fan, that she is pretentious and vain, that she has some concern for possible dangers to the happiness of her young mistress and that she loves intrigue (she probably brought Paris into the conversation only to arouse Romeo's jealousy). We also learn that she is not above accepting a bribe. We shall not be surprised to find her dishonest, even treacherous, later.

ACT II · SCENE 5

Question 1.
What is noticeable about the time of day of this scene and the last?

Answer
In Scene 4, "the hand of the dial is now upon the prick of noon." But, early in this scene, it is still 12 o'clock. It would appear, then, that time has stood still, yet, all through the play, we receive an impression of rapid action.

Question 2.
Criticize the nurse's behavior in this scene.

Answer
Her sour face and her delay in giving her message cannot be sufficiently accounted for by the breathlessness and slowness natural to old age, as she claims. She is the privileged old family servant and she loves to show her authority. But there is something petty and mean in the pleasure she takes in keeping Juliet in suspense. She deliberately tortures one she loves.

Question 3.
How can this scene be compared with that of Romeo's discussion with the friar?

Answer
Both scenes contrast the impatience of youth with the careful slowness of old age. The friar's age and experience have given him wisdom and taught him the advantages of cautious action stemming from sound reasoning. The nurse's years have only made her more tiresome, slow and self-important. However, in both scenes, the older person serves as contrast for the youthful impulsiveness of the lovers.

ACT II · SCENE 6

Question 1.
What is the dramatic purpose of this scene?

Answer
Although we see no celebration of marriage on the stage, this may be regarded as the marriage scene. The friar has delivered his sermon, Romeo and Juliet have expressed their enthusiastic consent and Friar Laurence has said he "will make short work" of the rest. When the next scene opens, we know that Romeo and Juliet are married.

Question 2.
How does this scene hint at future misfortune?

Answer
The friar no longer speaks of the good that may result from the marriage of Romeo and Juliet. Instead, he begins by praying "that after-hours with sorrow chide us not." The friar also repeats the warning against reckless, hurried action: "Too swift arrives as tardy as too slow." Such remarks foreshadow the sorrow that will follow the marriage of these "star-cross'd lovers."

ACT III · SCENE 1

Question 1.
At what time of year does the play take place?

Answer
In this scene, Benvolio speaks of "these hot days" when the mad blood is stirring. In Act I, Scene 1, we learned that Lammas-tide (August 1) was to be in "a fortnight and odd days." Notice, also, that the nurse cannot stir without her fan. Clearly, mid-July is indicated, not springtime, as is commonly thought.

Question 2.
Comment on Mercutio's description of Benvolio.

Answer
In this ironical description of Benvolio, Mercutio evidently

is drawing a picture of his own character. Benvolio has a mild, cautious disposition, not the quarrelsome nature that Mercutio describes.

Question 3.
Why does Tybalt wish to fight with Romeo? Why does Mercutio fight with Tybalt?

Answer
Tybalt saw Romeo, a Montague, speaking with his cousin, Juliet, at the masquerade. Tybalt wanted to challenge him on the spot. Being prevented from doing so by Capulet, he had sent a written challenge, to which he had received no satisfactory reply. Therefore, he goes in search of Romeo to provoke him to fight.

Mercutio, though not a Montague and not a bully like Tybalt, is, nevertheless, a man of honor and a born fighter. He cannot understand Romeo's calm and apparently dishonorable submission. Having no knowledge of the reasons for Romeo's peaceful attitude, he fights for the honor of his friend.

Question 4.
How could Romeo have prevented Mercutio's death?

Answer
Had Romeo confided to his friends his love for Juliet, Mercutio would not have continued the quarrel with Tybalt and probably would have used his wit to save Romeo honorably from his dangerous dilemma.

Question 5.
Why is the death of Mercutio a dramatic necessity?

Answer
Until now, and especially in the later scenes, Mercutio has monopolized much of the attention of the audience. He has fulfilled his purpose as a lively contrast to the melancholy and sentimental Romeo. From now on, the hero's dramatic importance grows with every scene. If Mercutio were allowed to live, he must either drop silently out of the play, or become a shadow of his former self. It is better, therefore, that he should

die while at the height of his popularity with the audience than that he should simply drop out of the picture.

The death of Mercutio is also necessary in that it provokes Romeo to kill Tybalt in revenge. This leads to Romeo's banishment and later complications in the plot.

ACT III · SCENE 2

Question 1.

What is an epithalamium? In what respects does Juliet's soliloquy resemble one?

Answer

An epithalamium is a marriage song, usually in praise of the bride or bridegroom, and praying for their prosperity.

One of the characteristics of the bridal song is its reference to mythological figures related to love, especially Hymen and Cupid. Another characteristic is that it contains a refrain, developing some leading image, and repeated at fixed or irregular intervals. These characteristics are found in Juliet's soliloquy. There is mention of Phœbus, Phæthon and Cupid, and, for the refrain, we have four appeals to night, occurring at almost regular intervals.

Question 2.

What effect does the nurse's mourning for Tybalt have on Juliet's grief and on the structure of the scene itself?

Answer

A refusal or inability to relate facts quickly and clearly is characteristic of the nurse. Here, this is again apparent. Juliet, newly married and impatiently waiting for the arrival of night and her husband, is led to believe that Romeo is dead, and the nurse does not immediately correct the assumption. Instead, the nurse selfishly continues her own moaning. The nurse, even in a tragic situation, reveals those characteristics that, under normal circumstances, make her comic.

Juliet's grief is deepened through this foreshadowing of the death of her husband. The difficulty of Juliet's situation is emphasized by the ambiguity introduced by the nurse. Initially, Juliet's grief arises from misunderstanding the nurse. Later, however, an understanding of the actual situation—that Tybalt is dead, and Romeo is responsible—complicates Juliet's situation even more.

ACT III · SCENE 3

Question 1.

Describe the attitudes of Romeo and the friar toward each other.

Answer

The attitude of Romeo toward the friar is one of grateful love, combined with the respect and obedience due to a spiritual director. Romeo addresses him as "my ghostly father," "blessed man," "my father" and with boyish confidence, runs to him for help in his every need. To the friar, Romeo is "pupil mine," and "my dear son," in whom "birth and heaven and earth do meet." He feels deep love and concern for the young man.

Question 2.

Compare the way in which Romeo reacts to the news of his banishment with Juliet's reaction.

Answer

Romeo receives the news from the friar. He is horrified and declares it to be worse than death. He vows that he cannot live away from Verona and Juliet. He refuses the friar's advice to think of the sentence philosophically or to hide when he supposes the knocking on the door to be the watchman to arrest him, preferring the death that would follow arrest. When he learns from the nurse of Juliet's grief, he draws his sword to kill himself and is restrained only by the suggestion that he wait in Mantua until the prince lifts his sentence.

The nurse takes the news of the banishment of Romeo and of Tybalt's death to Juliet. Juliet, under the double shock, first expresses anger against Romeo for killing her cousin. Then, when the nurse agrees with her condemnation of Romeo, Juliet calls herself a beast for criticizing him. She finds comfort in the thought that Romeo is still alive but, when she realizes what banishment means, she declares it worse than the death of

10,000 Tybalts, or the death of her parents, and she cries bitterly. But both Romeo and Juliet have accepted the punishment by the time they say good-bye in the second balcony scene.

ACT III · SCENE 4

Question 1.

Is Capulet's action in this scene consistent with his attitude during his first discussion with Paris in Act I, Scene 2?

Answer

In his earlier conversation with Paris, Capulet told him that Juliet was too young to marry and suggested that the eager young man:

Let two more summers wither in their pride
Ere we may think her ripe to be a bride.

Capulet, in this early scene, seems like a reasonable parent, who also recommends that Paris "get her heart./My will to her consent is just a part."

But now, Capulet approves Juliet's marriage to Paris and sets an early date for the wedding. When Juliet objects to the speedy marriage, her father disregards her feelings and continues the wedding plans without worrying about her consent.

ACT III · SCENE 5

Question 1.

What is a dawn song? Show that the dialogue in this scene is of this type.

Answer

The dawn song is a kind of dialogue poem between two lovers who have secretly spent the night together. The song usually relates to their reluctance to leave each other and their dread of discovery. As dawn approaches, they question whether the light comes from the sun or from the moon and whether the singing bird they hear is the nightingale or the lark.

The same pattern is used in the dialogue between Romeo and Juliet, but it is given added interest and urgency by the knowledge that Romeo's death is the price to be paid for too long a delay.

Question 2.
What does the nurse do to help the secret love of Romeo and Juliet?

Answer
She is Juliet's confidante and messenger in Act II, Scene 2 and Act IV, Scene 4. She tells Juliet, "I am the drudge, and toil in your delight." She brings the rope ladder (Act III, Scene 2) and, with it, news of Tybalt's death and Romeo's banishment. She cheers Juliet with news of Romeo (Act III, Scene 2) and seeks him out in the friar's cell (Act III, Scene 3), giving him the ring by which his "comfort is revived" and advising haste.

In this scene, she warns the lovers of Lady Capulet's approach. Later, however, when asked by Juliet for "some comfort, nurse," she hypocritically advises her to forget her banished lover and marry Paris, compared to whom "Romeo's a dishclout."

Question 3.
How does Juliet react to the nurse's advice to marry Paris?

Answer
At the end of this scene, Juliet rises to the height of heroism. When advised by the nurse to abandon Romeo for Paris, she turns against the "ancient damnation," the "most wicked fiend," and resolves to die rather than desert her lover. But, before resorting to death as a cure for her agony—which would be a weakness—she will ask the advice of Friar Laurence.

ACT IV · SCENE 1

Question 1.
How is Paris portrayed as a conventional suitor?

Answer
Paris' lukewarmness contrasts with the passionate intensity of Romeo's love for Juliet. Paris makes a few elegant speeches that have no deep feeling behind them. He relies upon his

position and dignity to win Juliet, whom he regards as a decorative possession: "Beauty too rich for use, for earth too dear." He bargains with Juliet's parents for her hand, but he makes no attempt himself to "stop the inundation of her tears."

Question 2.
Would Romeo and Juliet have been better off without the friar's assistance?

Answer
No. His refusal to help would probably have landed them in worse troubles. Nothing he could have done would have put an end to their passionate love. Had he not married them, they would have taken illegitimately what was lawfully denied them. He acted out of the best of motives. As Juliet says, (Act IV, Scene 3): "he hath still been tried a holy man." It is easy to be wise after the event. We know now that the friar's plans could never have healed a feud that had persisted through generations. But his reasoning, at the time, was sound.

ACT IV · SCENE 2

Question 1.
Why does Capulet move forward the wedding date of Paris and Juliet? What is the dramatic importance of the change?

Answer
He tends to change his mind, and he enjoys asserting his authority. He moves up the date of the marriage partly because of impatience in delaying a festivity, but chiefly because of Juliet's consent to marry Paris and fear that she may again refuse. Fate is also at work in his decision.

The dramatic effect is that it ruins the friar's plan to keep Romeo informed of conditions in Verona. The tragedy that occurs because the letter is not delivered could have been avoided if the friar had had another 24 hours to send Romeo a second letter.

ACT IV · SCENE 3

Question 1.
How does this scene heighten the dramatic impact of the play?

Answer
The dramatization of Juliet's taking the potion emphasizes the depth of her love, which strengthens her to commit an act of desperation.

Juliet's visions of waking up in the tomb, among the bones of her ancestors, with the ghost of Tybalt hunting for Romeo, foreshadow the final events in the Capulet vault.

Question 2.
What change does Juliet experience in this scene?

Answer
The audience, swept along by the story, is likely to forget that Juliet, though physically old enough to be married, is mentally still a child. Her emotions, therefore, shift from those of a girl just in her teens to those of a young woman in love. Here, we see the horrible imaginings of a frightened girl being overcome by the strong love of a faithful wife.

ACT IV · SCENE 4
Question 1.
Why has this scene been included in the play?

Answer
After Juliet drinks the potion, Shakespeare adds an ironic touch to the play by showing us the preparations for her marriage. As in the earlier scenes of domestic life at the Capulet home, this scene contributes a dimension of realism to the play. Thus, realism and romance combine to form a frequent pattern in the play.

ACT IV · SCENE 5
Question 1.
In what different ways do the mourners express themselves?

Answer
Capulet, who probably feels the greatest sorrow, is the most controlled in his expressions of grief. He also is the most poetic. After the friar's scolding of the mourners for their

excessive grief, Capulet's agony turns to more dignified acceptance. Lady Capulet's is the conventional sorrow that expresses itself in short exclamations and with much repetition. The nurse provides a characteristic echo, which she makes grotesquely comic. Paris is self-centered, considering himself wronged, spited and cheated out of his property.

Question 2.

What is the purpose of the scene between Peter and the musicians?

Answer

Shakespeare wrote plays not only to satisfy his own poetic and dramatic instinct, but also to attract and to please audiences. Therefore, he had to provide amusement. Scenes of grandeur or pathos were often mixed with passages of comedy or colorful spectacle. Moreover, there was no curtain to fall at the end of an act; instead, the division between acts was often indicated by conversations such as that between Peter and the musicians. The main purpose of this scene, therefore, is to indicate that the act is over, and to relieve the strain before the tragedy reaches a peak.

Question 3.

Outline the friar's criticism of the mourners.

Answer

The remedy for death is not in uncontrollable weeping, the friar tells them. The girl was given to them by heaven, and, now that she has been taken back, she is better off there than here. She would have had to die at some time, in any case. All that her parents desired was her well-being. Why should they mourn now that she has attained it fully? They are foolish to grieve for her when she is happy. The best marriage is the shortest. The friar then instructs them to lay their flowers on her and carry her to the church for burial.

ACT V · SCENE 1

Question 1.

Discuss the use of scenes of rapid contrast as a dramatic device in this play.

Answer

In this scene, Romeo's dream forecasting "some joyful news at hand" is closely followed by the entrance of Balthasar, bearing the news of Juliet's (supposed) death. Note the alternations of emotion: the love scene in Act II, Scene 2, followed by the calm philosophy of the friar in Act II, Scene 3, and the lively exchanges of wit and nonsense between Benvolio, Mercutio, Romeo and the nurse in Act II, Scene 4. In Act III, the violent duels are followed by Juliet's twilight soliloquy, soon to be interrupted by the confused and irritating speech of the nurse, bearing the news of Tybalt's death, followed by the calming sermon of the friar upon "adversity's sweet milk philosophy."

Question 2.

How does Romeo respond to the news of Juliet's death?

Answer

Romeo is no longer the dreamy poet he was three days before, no longer the prophet or the sentimentalist. He has become an energetic, determined man of action. His short, sharp, simple sentences show the depth and sincerity of his emotion. His mind is made up instantly: He will die by Juliet's side. The new forceful and practical side of his character is apparent in his orders to Balthasar and his reply to his servant's warning to him to have patience.

Question 3.

What indications are there in this scene that Romeo has matured?

Answer

He is now more manly, more determined and more intent on action. He seeks no guidance from others; when it is offered, he sternly brushes it aside. He is no longer acting out the role of a lover. He indulges in no self-questioning and he bravely challenges fate and defies the stars. His imagination has matured; he could not, a day or two earlier, have said:

There is thy gold, worse poison to men's souls,
Doing more murder in this lothsome world,

Than these poor compounds that thou mayst not sell:
I sell thee poison, thou has sold me none

This speech shows a cynical, realistic attitude that Romeo, a few days earlier, could not have expressed.

ACT V · SCENE 2

Question 1.
What is the importance of this scene?

Answer
This brief scene is essential because Friar Laurence must be told that Romeo is not yet aware of the true circumstances of Juliet's "death." The friar must now hurry to the tomb, where he will clear up the situation for the two families in the end.

ACT V · SCENE 3

Question 1.
Compare Romeo's farewell at the tomb with Juliet's. Suggest reasons for their difference.

Answer
Romeo is concerned about nothing but killing himself at Juliet's side and he displays little emotion. He carries Paris' body into the vault and speaks to it at some length before he even looks at Juliet. When he notices Juliet, his first thought is how beautiful she is in death, and, since death is so beautiful, he will join her in it. He embraces her, kisses her, addresses his poisonous drink and takes it.

Juliet wakens from her sleep in a cheerful mood at sight of the friar. On hearing of Romeo's death, she shows controlled emotion, searches unsuccessfully for the poison he has taken and, then, hearing a noise outside, takes his dagger and kills herself.

Juliet's more practical nature prompts her to act quickly in killing herself. Romeo, the more sentimental of the two, lingers to comment on the sadness of Paris' death and the beauty of Juliet.

Question 2.
Is any dramatic purpose served by the death of Paris?

Answer

Shakespeare's audiences enjoyed witnessing fights and duels on the stage and they took the same sort of critical interest in them that many of us do in a sporting event. Apart from this, the death of Paris seems unnecessary. It does not throw any further or clearer light on the chief character. Although it shows that Romeo's character has developed since he was confronted by Tybalt and called a villain to his face, this development has already been proved and needs no further emphasis. But the fight does provide an outlet for Romeo's excitement, so that he is able, afterward, to deliver calmly the beautiful speech before his own death.

Question 3.

In what different ways is death pictured in Romeo's last speech?

Answer

Death is described as a honeybee, a besieged fortress, a lover, a lean, horrible monster, a lawyer and a desperate pilot.

Question 4.

How have inevitable delays led to disaster in this scene?

Answer

There has been, first, the unforeseen delay of Friar John with the letter that would have saved both Romeo and Juliet. Now, the friar's stumbling progress to the tomb is another delay that has fatal results. If he had arrived a moment earlier, he would have found Romeo alive. Had the page summoned the watchman an instant sooner, Juliet's life would have been saved.

Question 5.

Show how reckless haste also leads to disaster.

Answer

A too-hasty servant tells Romeo that Juliet is dead (Act V, Scene 1), and Romeo too hastily believes the news. His head-strong recklessness leaves Friar Laurence no time to reach him by a second letter. Juliet's apparent obedience to her father's will prompts Capulet to move forward the marriage by a day (Act IV, Scene 2). This difference of a day makes the difference between life and death.

Question 6.

Why does Shakespeare continue the play after the death of Juliet?

Answer

Shakespeare still has to show that the love of Romeo and Juliet triumphs in the end over:

> the continuance of their parents' rage
> Which, but their children's end, nought could remove.

There are additional matters taken care of in the final lines. The confusion of the last scenes requires clearing up, and Shakespeare accomplishes this through the friar's plain and simple explanation. Also, the families' promise to raise statues of gold to the lovers leaves us with an impression of peace and harmony by adding a saintly image to the glory of the hero and heroine.

Part C: General Review Questions and Answers

Question 1.

In what year was *Romeo and Juliet* probably written? Base your answer on evidence from the play itself.

Answer

The exact date of the composition of *Romeo and Juliet* is unknown. It is now usually assigned to the year 1591, though some authorities think it may not have been written before 1595.

The chief reason for giving 1591 as the date of composition of the tragedy is to be found in the play itself. The nurse, in Act I, Scene 3, discussing Juliet's age with Lady Capulet, says:

On Lammas-eve at night shall she be fourteen;
That shall she, marry; I remember it well.
'Tis since the earthquake now eleven years.

There was an earthquake in London on April 6, 1580, in which chimneys fell down, and houses were destroyed. It is not unreasonable to assume that Shakespeare is referring to this earthquake and that he wrote the lines 11 years later, 'for the event made a great impression when it happened and would still be fresh enough in the minds of most of the audience. Such references to recent or contemporary events are found in many of his plays, but they cannot always be understood today because of our lack of knowledge of the history of the times. It is also worth noting in this connection that there is no mention of any earthquake in any of the possible sources of the play.

Question 2.

What sources did Shakespeare use for the play? How does Shakespeare's play differ from the material on which it is based?

Answer

Three distinct sources were used by Shakespeare in the composition of the play. The most important was Arthur Brooke's poem, written in 1562, called *The Tragicall Hystory of Romeus and Juliet, containing a rare Example of true Con-*

stancie: with the subtill Counsels and Practices of an old Fryer, and their ill event. This poem, composed in rhymed iambic verses of 12 and 14 syllables alternately, supplied the foundation of Shakespeare's play. The story was not new when Arthur Brooke wrote his poem. It already had a history dating from the second century. A second source was provided by a French translation of Matteo Bandello's story of Romeo and Julietta, made, with some variations, by Pierre Boisteau in 1559. It was from this French translation that Arthur Brooke produced his lyrical version of the story, with additional detail. A third source was a prose translation of Boisteau's novel, made in 1567 by William Painter, and entitled *Rhomeo and Julietta.*

A play of *Romeo and Juliet* is known to have existed before 1562, and there is some evidence that it was popular in its day, but all trace of it has been lost. This earlier play is referred to by Brooke in his "Address to the Reader," a sort of moralizing introduction to his poem. Shakespeare may have seen the earlier play on the stage or read it in manuscript.

Shakespeare followed Brooke's poem closely for his plot. The incidents are much the same in the play and the poem, except that, in the poem, Paris does not visit the tomb and, consequently, is not killed by Romeo. From Painter, Shakespeare may have taken some details for the character of Tybalt. The poem gives no indication how long Juliet will be affected by the sleeping drug, but, in Painter's version of the tale, the friar tells Juliet she shall remain unconscious "the space of forty hours at the least."

Shakespeare's most important change in the plot, from a dramatic point of view, is the speeding-up of the progress of events after the marriage of Romeo and Juliet. In the poem, the lovers are happily married for three months. In the play, Tybalt is killed by Romeo on the very day of the marriage. In the poem, Romeo is still alive when Juliet awakes from her torpor, but, having already taken poison, he explains his fatal error and then falls to the ground. Juliet closes his eyes and weeps. Determined to die with him, she forces her breathing to stop, and finally lets out a piercing shriek before falling dead upon her husband's corpse. The poem ends with the retirement of the friar to a hermitage, the banishment of the nurse and the execution of the apothecary.

Mercutio is almost entirely Shakespeare's creation. For the

nurse, Shakespeare borrowed from the poem only her characteristic traits of talkativeness and lack of principle. The friar of the play is quite a different person from the "grosse unlearned foole" of the poem. But it is in the characterization of Shakespeare's hero and especially of his heroine that his genius is most evident. Juliet, in the poem, is "scarce yet full sixteen years—too young to be a bryde." Bandello and Painter both speak of her as being 18 years old. In the poem, she is sophisticated and deceitful. Shakespeare has given both Romeo and Juliet the charm of delicacy and innocence and created in their love a pathos and a beauty that are altogether absent from the poem.

Question 3.

Discuss the development and motivation of Romeo and Juliet as characters in the tragedy.

Answer

The love of Romeo and Juliet for each other never changes. From the first moment of the sonnet-encounter and from their meeting soon after in the Capulet garden, there is no progression in their relationship. It is an absolute in the dramatic action, and its ideal nature provides the basis of their existence. In this sense, then, one might say that there is no development in their love. In the brief space of time of the tragedy, Romeo and Juliet never lessen the intensity found in the first scenes of their love. Juliet vows that she will have her wedding bed as a grave if Romeo is married. Romeo immediately climbs the Capulet wall, an invitation to certain death, as Juliet warns him in the balcony scene. Their suicides at the end of the tragedy, therefore, are simply logical developments from this same intensity of love.

In another sense, however, the lovers do develop and they show this development through their response to the forces of society and fate that burden their love. Romeo has his deepest attack of love melancholy in Friar Laurence's cell after he learns of his exile. He is at his manliest when he has fulfilled his love on his wedding night and must flee. After that point, his strange quietness and abruptness (notice his brief response to the news of Juliet's "death") prove that the center of his existence, his love, has intensified and tightened. He can act only in response to that love. Certainly this mature Romeo is a different creature from the Romeo of the first scene, the romantic idealist. The two contrasting kinds of melancholy, one almost a joke and the other an encounter with death in the Capulet tomb, reveal the tightening of character in Romeo. This intensification is the result of Romeo's response to outward circumstance, and it is a marked development. Finally, this development reveals itself most obviously, as does so much of the play, in the language. The artificial and extravagant phrases of the first scenes still appear in Romeo's speeches to death in the last scene, but the artificiality is justified by the truth of the dramatic situation. The language, therefore, becomes moving because Romeo is now faced with his own death.

Juliet shows this same development in her almost maternal protection of their love. Her love, she said at the Capulet feast, had a "prodigious birth." She, therefore, endures any hardship or test to protect her love. Her most terrifying scene is the moment when she is deserted by father, mother and, finally, her nurse. At that moment, her isolation is apparent and the girl she was at the beginning of the tragedy, surrounded and protected by Lady Capulet and her nurse, has vanished forever. Finally, the complete desperation and maturity required for the taking of the drug is the dramatization of her development. One would have expected of this practical girl such a possibility of violent action. But her suffering is proof of the development of her character as it changes to protect the center of her existence, her love for Romeo. This center is static, but her character protecting that center changes and isolates itself more and more to protect that center. Self-destruction becomes her ultimate means of protecting her love.

Question 4.

Contrast the characters of Romeo and Juliet.

Answer

Juliet is practical, unselfish, capable of practising deceit when the need for it arises and ready to take the lead on all important occasions. Romeo, on the other hand, is romantic, idealistic, high-strung, a poor actor with little command over his emotions and ready to submit his will to the stronger will of Juliet. The contrast is made particularly obvious in one or two scenes; first, in the garden scene, at their first private meeting, and again in the friar's cell. In the latter scene, Romeo loses all self-control. "With his own tears made drunk," he acts "like a misbehaved and sullen wench." He will not listen to reason, but, in a state of temporary insanity, thinks only of taking his own life. Juliet, on the other hand, also overcome with grief is able to take useful action. Her case is worse than Romeo's, for she is threatened, not only with separation from him, but with a hated and impossible marriage and with her parents' anger. But in the friar's cell, she shows as much bravery as Romeo has shown despair. Meeting Paris, she hides her feelings of despair. Then, she bravely and eagerly accepts the friar's plan.

In their deaths, too, Juliet shows greater courage. Romeo is too hasty to consider Juliet's lifelike appearance before taking the poison. Juliet, with few words and in spite of the friar's warning to her to flee with him, stabs herself—a more courageous and terrible means of death than poison.

Question 5.
Describe the character of Romeo.

Answer
It is customary to think of Romeo as being one person before he fell in love with Juliet and quite a different person afterward. This is not necessarily true. Love transforms him, but his character does not undergo a fundamental change. When first we meet him, he is ripe for love and imagines himself deeply in love. Being imaginative, poetic and romantic, he indulges in the illusion of an immature heart. Then, the friar scolds him "for doting, not for loving." At this stage, he glories in his emotions, considers himself poorly treated, mopes, confides in friends of his own age, distrusts his parents and pours out his soul to the sympathetic friar. In short, he is a fairly ordinary youth, who is impulsive, reserved, charming and lacking determination or purpose in life. He sees clearly the stupidity of the feud between his family and that of the Capulets and regrets it, but he does nothing to end it. He sees "pathways to his will," but does not follow them.

His falling in love with Juliet and the death of Mercutio are the two crises in his life that seem to make him a changed man. Basically, he is the same, but passion strengthens him.

Resolution takes the place of irresolution, and he becomes a determined, active and passionate man, who disregards obstacles or eliminates them.

The innocence of both lovers is one of their most charming characteristics. Romeo's wooing begins with words that are filled with admiration and respect. He follows them up with action, mixing his action with beautiful poetry, sincere compliment and heartfelt vows. He gains the support of the friar and then the favor of the nurse. He is handsome, possessing a face "better than any man's," a leg that "excels all men's," a hand, and a foot, and a body "past compare." He shows boldness, poetic imagination, tenderness and generosity.

The death of his friend, Mercutio, brings out in Romeo qualities that were hidden before. On Tybalt's return after Mercutio's death, Romeo suddenly grows violent and exclaims:

> Alive, in triumph! and Mercutio slain!
> Away to heaven, respective lenity,
> And fire-eyed fury be my conduct now!

His killing of Tybalt and consequent banishment weaken him for a time. But another meeting with Juliet restores his courage, and, in Mantua, he rises to true manhood. On receiving news of Juliet's death, he becomes almost heroic.

Question 6.
Compare Romeo in love with Rosaline with Romeo in love with Juliet.

Answer
The friar was probably right when he said that Romeo's love for Rosaline "did read by rote and could not spell." It was conventional; there was little meaning behind Romeo's words. Although he thought he was in love with Rosaline, he was, in reality, in love with love, and his conduct was that of the conventional lover, characterized by sighs and a desire for solitude and secrecy. It was a mental distraction that led to no determined action or effort.

His attitude changes after he meets Juliet. His character is developed by true love. He no longer broadcasts his love, not even to his closest friends. He still indulges in flights of artificial language, but he is no longer content with this. He seeks the friar again, but, this time, not to moan about his love or to praise her. Romeo now has a practical purpose in mind:

> this I pray,
> That thou consent to marry us to-day.

Question 7.
Is melancholy Romeo's tragic flaw?

Answer
From the first scene of the play, the audience is made aware of Romeo's melancholy. Later, Romeo is advised by Benvolio to cure this dangerous passion through finding a new love. He does, and the result is intensification of love, rather than release from the passion. Mercutio's main function is his desire to tease Romeo out of this dangerous state. Probably the clearest scene in which love melancholy expresses itself occurs in Friar Laurence's cell, when Romeo learns of his exile. His excessive despair is harshly criticized by Friar Laurence, who attacks such a dangerous passion. Finally, the melancholy is seen in Romeo's address to death in the tomb scene and in the violence revealed in his murdering Paris. Obviously, Shakespeare intends the audience to see Romeo as a slave of passion, lost in its demands and finally killing himself for love. Melancholy does operate, therefore, in the tragedy like the *hamartia*, or tragic flaw, that Aristotle defined as the defect within the hero that brings his downfall. Love melancholy, which the Elizabethans understood in a medical sense as well as in a moral and ethical one, was a dangerous passion. The conventional background of the idea that passion could be dangerous lay in the classical belief in the necessity for reason to rule over passion. A human being who has submitted the noble powers of reason to "rude will," as Friar Laurence calls it, or passion, could only find death. Love melancholy does operate in the tragedy, then, as Romeo's tragic flaw.

Question 8.
Where and how does Juliet reveal her practical nature?

Answer
We receive the first indication of her practical side at the

masked ball. Not wishing the nurse to know in whom she is particularly interested, she asks the names of two or three others before asking who Romeo is.

From the window above Capulet's orchard, Juliet, in the dialogue with Romeo, is full of curiosity and anxiety. She wants to know first *how* he came there and then *why*:

> How camest thou hither, tell me, and wherefore?
> The orchard walls are high and hard to climb,
> And the place death, considering who thou art,
> If any of my kinsmen find thee here.

Romeo answers in dreamy, abstract language. The conversation that follows is an exchange of practical realism on her part and airy romance on his. She thinks of the practical aspects of their situation: a plan is to be decided upon; they must not risk another interview; they will marry secretly and leave Verona. She shows a certain amount of caution:

> If that thy bent of love be honourable,
> Thy purpose marriage, send me word to-morrow,
> By one that I'll procure to come to thee,
> Where and what time thou wilt perform the rite.

To make sure of Romeo's sincerity, she asks the question that, in other circumstances, a mother would have asked.

In all her subsequent actions, she is ruled by practical demands. Perhaps when the friar advises her to pretend to consent to the marriage with Paris, though, she overplays the part, confessing that she has sinned, begging pardon and promising to be ruled by her father from now on.

Question 9.

Describe the nurse's character.

Answer

We have evidence of the nurse's talkative nature almost every time she opens her mouth. Juliet's age is in question; the nurse requires 25 lines to say that she will be 14 in about two weeks (Act I, Scene 3). When sent by Juliet to learn from Romeo where and when he has arranged for the marriage, she talks for more than 100 lines (Act II, Scene 4), saying the same thing over and over again, until Romeo is utterly confused. She interrupts and introduces all sorts of irrelevant topics and spends three hours on an errand that she promised to do in half an hour. When she returns to Juliet, her wandering speech, repetitions and excuses so frustrate Juliet that she exclaims in anger:

> The excuse that thou dost make in this delay
> Is longer than the tale thou dost excuse.
> Is thy news good or bad? Answer to that.

The nurse's account of Tybalt's death is so confused and accompanied by such roundabout information that Juliet is unable to figure out who is dead:

> What storm is this that blows so contrary?
> Is Romeo slaughter'd, and is Tybalt dead?

That the nurse can keep a secret is shown by the fact that Juliet never has to swear her to secrecy, yet her meetings with Romeo are kept from her mother's knowledge. The nurse, however, asks Romeo to vouch for the secrecy of his man. She thus illustrates the saying:

> Two may keep counsel, putting one away.

Her instinctive love of intrigue and secrecy is apparent when she says to Romeo, when sent to him with a message, "As I told you, my young lady bade me inquire you out; what she bade me say, I will keep to myself."

Her hypocrisy is best seen in her change of attitude toward Romeo after receiving the bribe and in the scene in which she imitates Juliet, who, in a moment of great distress, condemns Romeo, and in the way in which she deserts Romeo when Juliet's parents plan her wedding to Paris, the gentleman to whom "Romeo's a dishclout." As for the nurse's insolence, much of her conversation with both Lady Capulet and Juliet, containing many indecent expressions or anecdotes, is apparently received without surprise by those to whom it is addressed. But when she calls her master "cot-quean" (Act IV,

Scene 4), she is certainly taking liberties for a servant.

She is trusted by Lady Capulet, whose trust she betrays. In the presence of Juliet, she is all for Romeo, but to Lady Capulet she is equally enthusiastic about Paris. She accepts a bribe from Romeo and later turns against him. But she is devoted to Juliet and is at her best when she stands up boldly to Capulet.

Question 10.
What is the nurse's dramatic function in the play?

Answer
Obviously, the nurse was intended by the dramatist, first of all, to provide comic relief and, secondly, as a background to Juliet.

She has been chiefly responsible for the training of Juliet, and we ask ourselves what sort of influence she can have had on the child to whom she was so closely attached and so genuinely devoted. The result of her training is shown in the freedom with which Juliet expresses thoughts and emotions that young girls usually keep secret. Evidently the nurse has always been as free in conversation with Juliet as she is with her mistress and her master. She never minces words. She gives herself full credit for having influenced Juliet:

> Were not I thine only nurse,
> I would say thou hadst suck'd wisdom from thy teat.

The result is that, in Juliet, we see the effect of free and loose talk upon perfect, natural refinement.

The nurse is a willing go-between, carrying messages from Juliet to Romeo and back again.

> I am the drudge, and toil in your delight

she says, as she goes to bring a rope ladder. She is even a necessary means of communication between Lady Capulet and her daughter, who, apparently, do not have a close relationship. She uses her privileges as an ancient family servant to speak her mind to old Capulet more boldly than his wife dares. In fact, she runs the Capulet house on the domestic side.

She is at the same time mean and good-natured, loyal and

treacherous, ignorant and worldly wise—a mass of contradictions, yet perfectly true to life.

Question 11.
Discuss the nurse as a stock character.

Answer
A stock character is usually a conventional character and may often be a static character—that is, one who does not show development as the play progresses. The nurse is based on the obscene old woman who was a common figure in the Roman comedy of Plautus and Terence. She also functions like the servants in Roman comedy, who act as go-betweens for the major characters. Those scenes in which she delays telling Juliet key information are scenes ultimately derived from Roman comedy. The important point is that Shakespeare took such a stock character from ancient traditions and gave it the lift that only old Angelica—a name ringing with irony—has in all of English literature. Her coarseness serves a vital schematic purpose in the drama; her realistic language heightens the lyric language of the lovers by providing ironic contrast, and her farcical actions, although derived from Roman comedy, are completely English slapstick and perform an important function in the dramatic construction of the tragedy.

Question 12.
What part is taken in the play by Prince Escalus?

Answer
The prince serves as a bridge between the feuding families. He is above and outside the quarrels that form the basis of the tragedy. He represents law and justice—tempered with mercy—while the other characters break the law. Always about at the right moment, in the first act he orders the heads of the opposing households to keep the peace. In the third act, he sets up an inquiry into the deaths of Mercutio and Tybalt and, "rushing aside the law," decrees banishment instead of death for Romeo. The last occasion of his appearance is when he is sent for to unravel the mystery of three deaths. His final speech to Montague and Capulet supplies the key to the tragedy and

points to the fulfilment of the promise made in the first prologue. He asks ironically:

Where be these enemies? Capulet! Montague!

and adds:

See, what a scourge is laid upon your hate,
That heaven finds means to kill your joys with love!
And I, for winking at your discords too,
Have lost a brace of kinsmen; all are punish'd.

Question 13.
What is Benvolio's dramatic function?

Answer

Benvolio is a good example of a static, stock character. He functions to suggest the bachelor background of Romeo, to serve as a backdrop to the view of the young lover as a social creature with friends and family. His remarks in the various scenes with Romeo and Mercutio often serve as contrasts to Mercutio's and Romeo's jokes or statements. He is gentler with Romeo than Mercutio is because he tends to understand Romeo's desire to seek the night (there is an implication in his first speech that he too has known love melancholy) and the feelings of the lovesick. But he is just as determined to rid Romeo, his dear friend and cousin, of this dangerous illness. It is his plan, ironically, that rids Romeo of Rosaline and leads him into the arms of Juliet. When Shakespeare no longer needs a foil for Romeo, he drops Benvolio. The last we see of this faithful friend is in Act III, when he advises Romeo to escape before he is caught and punished for killing Tybalt.

Question 14.
Sketch the characters of Mercutio and Benvolio.

Answer

Mercutio's character is drawn with distinctness and individuality. What he says is always characteristic and could have been said by no other person.

As a contrast to Romeo, Mercutio is the complete realist,

hating pretence and all new fashions (Act II, Scene 4). Romeo is an idealist. Mercutio is scornful of love and of dreams and visions; Romeo lives in his imagination, is swayed by dreams he has had and sees nothing by the pure light of reason. Mercutio is sensual, while Romeo is a romantic to whom love is a matter of life and death, a "bright angel." Mercutio is all for action and sport, but Romeo is active only on impulse or when driven to action.

Mercutio overflows with animal spirits and gaiety. His wit is sometimes coarse and rude, but never unkindly. His liveliness never leaves him. Nothing is too slight for a jest and nothing so serious, not even his own death, that he cannot joke about it. His wit is a sort of dazzling self-entertainment. He is a born caricaturist in words. Without effort, he indulges in puns, quibbles and every kind of figure of speech—anything to raise a laugh. He lives for pleasure and sees the light and amusing side of everything.

He does not know fear. Duelling is, for him, no question of science or mathematics, as it is for Tybalt, but one of the pleasures of life. He enters into a quarrel with Tybalt simply because he cannot endure the sight of his friend refusing an opportunity to fight.

Benvolio is a rather characterless person. He may, however, be said to have three roles in the play: friend to Romeo; foil to Mercutio and Tybalt; and commentator.

As a pacifist, he is always cautious. He tries to distract Romeo from his first love, Rosaline, a Capulet; he hurries him away from the banquet, sensing a new danger in Juliet, perhaps; he tries to keep the peace whenever there is a fight or a likelihood of one. To Mercutio, he is "grand-sire" because he tries to throw the cold water of reason on the hot blood of passion or hate.

He is not cowardly, however. In the first scene, he fights with Tybalt until the battle is ended by the officers.

Question 15.

What part in the play is taken by Mercutio? What purposes are served by it?

Answer

Mercutio first appears with the maskers, when he delivers

his Queen Mab speech and persuades Romeo to take part in the dance and reconsider his idea of being merely a torchbearer. He next appears with Benvolio in search of Romeo after the dance. On the following morning, the same two are again in search of Romeo, who at last comes and jokes with them. The nurse enters, and the jesting continues at her expense. Mercutio's last appearance is when he is killed. He refuses to follow Benvolio's advice to leave the street, challenges Tybalt when he happens to come along and is killed as Romeo tries to part them.

His purpose is to add humor to the play by the display of his wit, to contrast his liveliness with Romeo's moodiness and to supply the means by which Shakespeare presents the highly poetic and imaginative Queen Mab speech. His being killed by Tybalt when Romeo interferes so angers the latter that he kills Tybalt out of revenge.

Question 16.

What is Paris' function? Why is he killed at the end of the play?

Answer

Paris helps to develop the central action and to provide a kind of counterpart to a major character—in this case, Romeo. It should be remembered, first of all, that he is neither Capulet nor Montague. He is, in fact, Mercutio's kinsman, a member of the prince's family. He genuinely loves Juliet, a fact proved by his constant pursuit of her, by his loving dialogue with her at Friar Laurence's cell and, most clearly, by his devotion at her tomb. His touching elegy and his desire to purify her tomb and keep watch over it are evidence of his love for Juliet. Therefore, Romeo is right when he calls him "brother" in this last scene.

But why should he be killed? Critics have found it a problem in the play, for the death is Shakespeare's own invention; it occurs in none of the other versions. It seems that Romeo's violence, later to be used against himself, is aroused when he quickly kills Paris. The violence of that death seems to heighten Romeo's state of despair at the tomb and complete the result of his love melancholy.

Question 17.

Sketch the characters of Capulet and Lady Capulet.

Answer

Capulet is hospitable: at the feast, he shows all the qualities of a kind and cheerful host, who finds his own pleasure in the enjoyment of others. Even the death of his nephew, Tybalt, does not prevent him from preparing to make his daughter's wedding an occasion of much festivity (Act IV, Scenes 2 and 4).

As a father, he expects ready obedience from his daughter. Though he says to Paris at one time, "My will to her consent is but a part," he is more sincere when he says later:

> I think she will be ruled
> In all respects by me; nay more, I
> doubt it not.

His method of gaining her consent is indicated a little later, when, in response to her prayers to him to be patient, he calls her a "disobedient wretch" and commands her:

> Speak not, reply not, do not answer me
> My fingers itch.

Yet, in his own way, he loves his daughter:

> The earth hath swallowed all my hopes
> but she.

When she pleases him, she is nothing worse than "headstrong" and "this same wayward girl." When he thinks her dead, he says, "And with my child my joys are buried," and expresses that beautiful simile:

> Death lies on her like an untimely frost
> Upon the sweetest flower of all the field.

Enough has been said to show that he is impulsive, hasty, unreasonable, willful, kindly when not crossed, and violent and even brutal when his will is opposed. But he is the first to hold out the hand of fellowship to his old enemy: "O brother Montague, give me thy hand."

Lady Capulet is a much less agreeable character. She is

cold-hearted, ambitious for social advancement, calculating, unsympathetic and vengeful. She neglects her daughter, whom she never attempts to understand. She abandons Juliet in her hour of extreme suffering (Act III, Scene 5) and speaks of a desire to see Romeo poisoned, "That he shall soon keep Tybalt company." Her grief at Juliet's supposed death is conventional. When Juliet really dies, Lady Capulet is chiefly concerned at the reminder that she is growing old:

> O me! this sight of death is as a bell
> That warns my old age to a sepulchre.

Question 18.
Compare the characters of Capulet and Montague.

Answer
The Capulets are more responsible for the feud than the Montagues. It is their servants who provoke the first street quarrel, and Tybalt deliberately seeks a duel with Romeo. Capulet calls for his sword when he first enters and lays his hands on Montague, who refuses to fight. Capulet is violent in language, while Montague is restrained. Capulet's grief over the deaths of Tybalt and Juliet is noisy, though not deep, while Montague's over Romeo is silent and deep. At the close of the play, Capulet is the first to seek reconciliation because of his outgoing nature, while Montague quietly agrees to the offer of peace by practically offering the statue in memory of Juliet. Capulet cannot be outdone in generosity and he offers the same for Romeo.

Question 19.
Describe Friar Laurence and the part he plays in the tragedy.

Answer
The friar, in contrast to all the other characters of the play, is a holy, philosophical man who, though living in the seclusion of a cell, interferes in worldly matters with disastrous results, thus illustrating one of his own sayings:

> Virtue itself turns vice, being misapplied.

He is loved by Romeo and by Juliet and respected by all. An authority on herbs and their medicinal virtues, he turns his knowledge to a practical use in the play. He is Romeo's confidant. Having a simple, hopeful nature and thinking no evil, he is willing to aid the lovers:

> For this alliance may so happy prove,
> To turn your households' rancour to pure love.

In this innocent hope, he performs the ceremony of marriage:

> So smile the heavens upon this holy act
> That after-hours with sorrow chide us not!

Unfortunately, "after-hours" do "chide" them. Disasters begin immediately after his well-intentioned act and pursue the married couple to the end.

With all his goodness and his sympathy, he cannot quite enter into Romeo's feelings (Act III, Scene 3), and, notwithstanding his good intentions, his advice to Juliet to deceive her parents and the remedy he provides against her marriage with Paris both lead to disastrous results.

In the concluding scenes, we see him striving unsuccessfully to undo the unhappy consequences of his actions. His late arrival in the churchyard, and Juliet's strong determination opposed to his weaker will, cause his efforts to repair the damage or prevent further harm to fail.

Question 20.

What is the central action of *Romeo and Juliet*? How does the structure of the play reveal the development of this action?

Answer

The central action of *Romeo and Juliet* is the love of the two young people. It is never allowed to fade once the lovers have met each other in the first act. Neither ceases to believe in the absolute nature of their passion. Both are willing to go to any limits for their love, from the simplest scaling of a wall or a balcony to the agonies of drugs and deception and, finally, to suicide. Their love is complete within itself; it cannot be threatened from within because the lovers are religiously certain of their love. How, then, does Shakespeare develop a structure around such a center? Largely through the method of external conflict, which, in the structural development of the tragedy, serves to isolate the lovers, finally driving them to the point of complete isolation and death.

This conflict can be found on several levels: (1) the love-hate action; (2) the youth-age action; (3) the ideal-real love action; (4) the fate-free will action. The love of Romeo and Juliet, as the prologue tells us, is to be understood as a public event. Therefore, it must struggle with the hate of the lovers' families. The feud functions as the source of hatred in spite of which the love must survive. Tybalt represents the essence of this hatred. He is explained, in medical terms, as a victim of his "humor," of choler. But, as a character, he is one-dimensional, and that dimension is hatred. He is in the play for no other reason than to dramatize the feud of the Montagues and Capulets. This feud extends even to the lesser members of the two houses. Most tragically, even the citizens of Verona must struggle with this insane war so helplessly out of hand, and, finally, even the prince feels the effect of the hatred in the loss of his two kinsmen, Mercutio and Paris. Against this background of hate, then, the lovers are portrayed as creatures of irony that redeem, in their private love, the whole public society of Verona.

The youth of Romeo and Juliet is important because it emphasizes speed, which acts as one instrument of fate in the tragedy. To accentuate its importance, Shakespeare made Juliet younger than the girl in Brooke's poem, his source. Another manner of accenting this feature of age was to place the young lovers in a world ruled by old people. The Capulets and the Montagues cannot penetrate the meaning of such ideal love, or love that is not based on social or material gain. Only Friar Laurence can understand, but, as Romeo points out in Act III, Scene 3, the priest cannot understand the intensity of the young man's passion and ideal love. Again, the lovers are isolated.

The sexual realism dramatized by the nurse, Mercutio and the servants in the first scene tests the idealism of the love of Romeo and Juliet. These scenes of coarseness and cynicism not only provide comic relief, but actually make the audience, overwhelmed by the realism of physical love, believe in the love expressed by the poetry of the private encounters of the lovers.

Shakespeare's conflicting structure, therefore, allows the central dramatic action of their love, as expressed in heightened poetry, to be believed. Thus, the lovers are believed to be truly different, truly isolated from the other characters of the play.

Finally, they are isolated by their own fateful circumstances. Seeing each other as "stars," (that is, as creatures who can shape their own wills and who can make their own fate), Romeo and Juliet have, as their opponent, the "stars" of fate. The first prologue calls them "star-cross'd lovers," and Romeo, on learning of Juliet's death, declares that he will defy the "stars." The lovers, then, are structured against the forces of accident and chance, which fate controls. Their ultimate victory in death over the "stars" of fate makes them true "stars," or saints, as the prince calls them at the end of the play.

The result of all four levels of conflict is to give the structure of the tragedy, in which the main action of the love of Romeo and Juliet is revealed, a powerful effect of dramatic irony.

Question 21.

What are the crucial scenes in the play? Where is the turning point of the dramatic action?

Answer

There are three crucial scenes in the play. The whole of the first act builds to the encounter of the lovers at the Capulet feast. With this last scene of the first act should be included the balcony scene (Act II, Scene 2), which immediately follows the first meeting of Romeo and Juliet. These two scenes, considered as one, form the first of the crucial scenes. The second scene crucial to the development of the action is Act III, Scene 1, in which Mercutio is killed by Tybalt and then Tybalt is killed by Romeo. The third crucial scene is the last of the tragedy, the suicides of the two lovers. There are many other scenes that are important in furthering the dramatic action (for example, the wedding in Friar Laurence's cell) and also in completing the sequence of several events (for example, the wedding night and the poetic speeches of the lovers at dawn), but each of these three scenes is the logical climax of dramatic action. Each is carefully prepared for in Shakespeare's dramatic construction. The last scene reveals the whole purpose of the play: the sacrificial death that unites the feuding families and brings peace to the society of Verona. The turning point of the play occurs in Act III, Scene 1. With Mercutio's death, the play can no longer maintain comic elements of any length. The death of such a sympathetic character demands compensation, or revenge. Romeo, therefore, kills Tybalt, and his cry "O! I am fortune's fool." is his own recognition that "this day's black fate on more days doth depend;/This but begins the woe others must end." The only solution to the drama after this scene will be tragic. Romeo's love is now overcome by the power of the feud and fate itself.

Question 22.

How do Friar Laurence and Prince Escalus function in terms of the structure of the tragedy?

Answer

Prince Escalus appears only three times in the play, each time to quiet the disturbance to the social order of Verona caused by the Capulets and Montagues. His speeches dramatize his role as upholder of justice in Verona. He represents an outside, impersonal force that directs the society and is the ultimate reason behind the political order. But, ironically, he is powerless in his great authority. He is not severe enough in his initial punishment, and the feud breaks out again. The final result is that he, too, is drawn into the battle through the loss of his two kinsmen, Mercutio and Paris. Finally, it is not political justice but sacrificial love that changes the order of hate in Verona.

Friar Laurence clearly represents spiritual authority, the voice of inherited wisdom, in the tragedy. But there is a difference between the wisdom of Friar Laurence's words and the powerlessness of his own actions and perceptions in the tragedy. His warnings to Romeo about his passion are clearly Shakespeare's intellectual statements about Romeo's tragic flaw. His first soliloquy about the herbs he is gathering in the July dawn is also clearly an answer to the problem of Romeo's misuse of his reason, of his "virtue." He is also obviously Romeo's spiritual father, and Romeo, as he says when leaving the friar for the last time, genuinely loves his confessor. But the friar does not understand the passionate intensity of Romeo's love. Further, his abandonment of Juliet in the tomb, knowing that she, like Romeo, will commit suicide reveals his simple confusion, not moral weakness. If, therefore, he does seem absurd at times, one must also remember that he is the clear voice of spiritual authority, intending, through the union of the lovers, to save Verona. Like the prince, he functions as an ultimate authority in the play.

Question 23.
What are the three most important themes in the play?

Answer
Shakespeare presents the three themes, or levels of meaning of the tragedy, in the opening sonnet of the prologue: fate, society, and the private love of Romeo and Juliet. Everything in the play finds its meaning in the logical (one might almost say mathematical) relationship of these three themes. The force of fate is signalled throughout the play by an intricate series of prophetic visions experienced by the major characters, Romeo and Juliet, and also by Friar Laurence. None of the other characters makes these predictions, but their force is felt, ironically, in the various actions that appear as coincidences or accidents. For example, seeing the servant give Romeo the guest list of the Capulet feast, the audience, having heard from the prologue that the lovers will die, will feel the force of a forewarning in the dramatic irony of the event.

But the most insistent means by which the audience feels the power of fate is in Shakespeare's use of speed in the dramatic action. Literally the form of the play is a matter of time, as the prologue tells us, "two hours' traffic." Shakespeare continues this sense of whirling action in the fight of the servants, in Paris' urgent courtship of Juliet, in the instant love of the two lovers, in the reference to their youth, in the immediate exchange of vows in the Capulet orchard and the plans for marriage, in the swift exchange between Tybalt and Mercutio and the death of both, in Romeo's flight, in the hurried plans for the marriage with Paris, in the suddenness with which Romeo learns of Juliet's "death" and, finally, in the speed of the events in the Capulet tomb. The characters always seem to be in a hurry, or acting for others who are in haste. This speed, then, forms dramatic evidence of the force of fate.

But the meaning of the play is not merely fatalistic. The prologue tells us that fate operates in the play as an instrument of providence. Of course, man has free will, as one of Friar Laurence's little sermons tell us. This "rude will" can dominate "grace," however: passion can overcome reason, or the voice of God in man, if passion is not controlled. The result is death, as Friar Laurence says in his speech in the second act. Fate *is* providence in *Romeo and Juliet*. As the prologue tells us, providence uses the instruments of fate to accomplish its own good ends—the renewal of the society of Verona. There is, therefore, a providence that can use accident and coincidence with all their terrible ironies for a specific end.

The Elizabethans believed that the universe was completely rational because God had created every bit of it with love. This is not to say that they thought it could be understood by man. But it is the obvious first meaning of *Romeo and Juliet* that providence uses the force of fate for its own ends.

Society is affected by the good ends of providence. Verona has been shaken by the bloody feud of the Montagues and Capulets, "where civil blood makes civil hands unclean." It is good to recall here that Shakespeare's tragedies are always public. Convention demanded that any serious action be displayed in the public realm. A private theme could never have enough relevance to be tragic. Therefore, Shakespeare sets up the second great theme in the public realm. The forces of family and political justice are set against the love of two teen-agers. Such great forces, with all their economic, political and social demands, crush the lovers in a few days.

The first scene shows even the servants involved in the feud. The discussion of Capulet and Paris shows how Juliet is really an economic possession. The social dimension is revealed fully in the Capulet feast and in the later preparations for the second wedding. The great importance of the family name is shown also in Juliet's immediate reaction to the news of Tybalt's death. These are a few of the many uses of the public dimension of the tragedy. Prince Escalus is the official voice of the suffering society of Verona. Friar Laurence, as its spiritual authority, seeks the wedding of Romeo and Juliet as a means of healing the wounds. Providence, however, acting through fate, is stronger than either of the two social voices. It has its own plan.

The third theme of the tragedy is the love between Romeo and Juliet. This force is an absolute, as already suggested. It is seemingly defeated by the immense pressures of fate and society. But love acts as a teacher to society. The belief of Romeo and Juliet in their ideal love is so absolute that it gives direction and meaning to both society and fate. Society is renewed by the absolute belief in love that Romeo and Juliet have. No great political, economic or socio-religious forces have been able to heal the feud and the hatred. The healing comes only from the love of two teen-agers, who have not yielded in their absolute devotion to the ideal of love. Even fate, with its instruments of accident and chance, is outwitted. Love, as revealed in the balcony scene and in the dawn farewells, is stronger than the force of coincidence. This third theme, then, of the ideal love of Romeo and Juliet is the real center of the tragedy, affected by the two forces of fate and society and itself affecting these two great forces.

Question 24.

How does Shakespeare dramatize the intensity of Romeo's and Juliet's love?

Answer

Shakespeare dramatizes this intense love through a skilful manipulation of conventional ideas. From the beginning, Romeo and Juliet address each other as saints (or pilgrims). Romeo is wearing a pilgrim's costume at the Capulet feast when he meets Juliet. This motif of the lovers as saints, introduced so lightly in the high comedy of the first scenes, works slowly through the tragedy until the final scene, when the sacrificial death of the lovers is revealed. Whatever the ultimate outcome of their suicide (damnation in the eyes of the church), their love has been a form of salvation. For these two lovers, therefore, both fathers will erect statues of pure gold and the entire city of Verona will pay tribute to them. In short, Romeo and Juliet have literally become saints in the little world of the play. Shakespeare has made the center of the play, the love, not only absolute in itself (by assuming the nature of holiness—a condition that an Elizabethan audience could believe in) but public and relevant to society. The imagery of sainthood has managed to suggest both the eternal and the earthly, and the social and private nature of their love. Like true saints, they have over-come death. The conventional meanings of the speeches to death that recur in the play, especially in the final scene in the Capulet tomb, are also put in the framework of the saint imagery. Death itself is subject to love. Their love, the scene implies, will overcome even death through its restorative powers. Ironically, in their death-marriage they will best serve life by redeeming it through sacrificial love, like true saints.

Question 25.
How is suspense developed in the play?

Answer
The tragedy is filled with suspense and tension. The quarrel between the servants of both houses arouses our interest from the beginning and makes it clear that more trouble is bound to arise from the situation. When Romeo and Juliet meet for the first time, it is evident that there are difficulties ahead of them. Tybalt's challenge to Romeo gives warning of conflict to follow. Even the calmness of the marriage scene gives the effect only of a lull in stormy proceedings. The first scene of Act III is filled with tension. Romeo comes straight from his marriage to be challenged by his new cousin, Tybalt. Tybalt's death and Romeo's banishment leave us in a state of anxiety as to the out-come. Capulet's discussion with Paris concerning his courtship of Juliet is the height of suspense, the audience being aware that, at that moment, Romeo and Juliet are together. Juliet's consent to try the friar's drug is bound to raise interest and expectation as to the result. Romeo's decision to take poison upon hearing of Juliet's death leads us to wonder whether tragedy can be avoided by some stroke of luck.

Question 26.
Comment on the element of superstition that appears throughout the play.

Answer
Dreams are referred to frequently in the play. We are not told Romeo's first dream (Act I, Scene 4—"I dreamed a dream to-night"), for that is the occasion for Mercutio to break in with his picturesque description of Queen Mab. When Romeo leaves

Juliet (Act III, Scene 5), she has a sort of prophetic vision: "I have an ill-divining soul!/Methinks I see thee, now thou art so low,/As one dead in the bottom of a tomb." When Romeo is in Mantua, waiting for news from the friar, he speaks of his dream:

> If I may trust the flattering truth of sleep,
> My dreams presage some joyful news at hand
> . . . .
> I dreamt my lady came and found me dead—
> Strange dream, that gives a dead man leave to think!—
> And breathed such life with kisses in my lips,
> That I revived and was an emperor.

The idea of an impersonal figure of justice, or fate, is brought into the prologue with the mention of "A pair of star-cross'd lovers." This idea is repeated through the play. In Act I, Scene 4, Romeo, speaking of attending the Capulet feast, says:

> "I fear, too early; for my mind misgives
> Some consequence, yet hanging in the stars,
> Shall bitterly begin his fearful date
> With this night's revels, and expire the term
> Of a despised life closed in my breast,
> By some vile forfeit of untimely death."

When Romeo kills Tybalt (Act III, Scene 1), he exclaims, "O! I am fortune's fool." The prince, in the final scene, exclaims, "Capulet! Montague!/See what a scourge is laid upon your hate,/That heaven finds means to kill your joys with love!"

Question 27.

Identify the various forms of verse used in *Romeo and Juliet*.

Answer

The tragedy has three levels of language: prose, blank verse and rhymed verse. With important exceptions, the prose is the language of servants and comedy; the blank verse is used for the personal and more intimate scenes (the love scenes, with their rhymes, are obvious exceptions); and the rhymed verse is used for the impersonal and generalized scenes. But, embedded within the tragedy are four conventional forms of lyric verse:

1) **Sonnet** There are three sonnets in the play. The chorus speaks the first in his prologue to Act I and the third sonnet in his prologue to Act II. The second sonnet occurs when Romeo and Juliet first meet at the Capulet feast. All three are examples of the English, or Shakespearean, sonnet, with the rhyme scheme of *abab, cdcd, efef, gg*—that is, three quatrains (four-line sections of a poem) and a couplet. The sonnet traditionally was used at this period for love poetry. It was derived from the Italian poet, Petrarch, whom Mercutio satirizes in the fourth scene of Act II.

2) **Epithalamium** Juliet's soliloquy, in the beginning of the second scene of Act III is an example of a wedding song, or epithalamium. She is praising her wedding and anticipating the consummation of her love that night. This is the traditional subject matter of an epithalamium, which, in English, can assume any metric form. Because this soliloquy is one of anticipation and waiting, it might also be called a serena, a poem recited in romances by the lady as she waits for her lover in the evening.

3) **Aubade** The dialogue of the two lovers in the dawn after their wedding night (the last scene of Act III) is an excellent example of a song sung at dawn, often as a mourning by lovers at the end of the night of love. This aubade, or dawn song, can have any metric form in English.

4) **Elegy** Paris' speech in the final scene, as he approaches Juliet's tomb and throws flowers over its entrance, is an example of a poem celebrating the dead, or an elegy. The poem could take any form in English, but here it is a simple rhymed lyric set into the blank verse of the scene.

Question 28.

Comment on the comedy in the play.

Answer

There are, generally speaking, two kinds of comedy in the play: the low comedy of the servants, ending usually in some sort of slapstick and farce, and the high comedy of wit and verbal duels. This first type of comedy is found in the first scene, the household scenes of the Capulet feast and the wedding preparations (both scenes involving important dramatic action), the scene in which Juliet's body is discovered (where Peter and the musicians joke) and the action of the cowardly page in the final scene. In every case, this kind of low comedy involving servants is based on Roman comedy and provides broad humor. It serves, in the structure and style, as comic relief to the almost unbearably tragic scenes that it often frames.

Between the two areas of high and low comedy lies the comedy of the nurse and Mercutio. The nurse tends to be part of the low comedy, but she is much more rounded as a character than, for example, Peter. She can suffer and she can give advice. But she, too, serves as a contrast with her crude, low comedy and her characteristics of an old peasant woman.

Mercutio naturally belongs to the level of high comedy because he possesses the gift of wit. But he, too, is involved in horseplay and the kind of active humor associated with farce, although it is his verbal wit and the sexual jokes that one best remembers. At the other end of high comedy, there is the verbal duelling of Romeo and Juliet in their various encounters. Progressively, their scenes together contain less of the lightness of lovers in Shakespeare's romantic comedies. But the sonnet at Capulet's feast does reveal an important side of both characters: their readiness to act in a social situation and to respond with intelligence to their own emotions. The audience needs to see these characters as rounded. Therefore, stylistically at least, they must first be presented as figures from a high comedy before their tragedy is unfolded. In both cases, the style of the play is intensified by the use of comedy, both low and high.

Question 29.

Briefly explain three dominant patterns of imagery in *Romeo and Juliet*.

Answer

The most comprehensive of all patterns of imagery is that contrasting light and darkness. Romeo seeks, says Benvolio, "artificial night." The night imagery is climaxed in the tomb scene, where, in the darkness of death, the lovers become a kind of eternal light to each other and to Verona. The balcony scene and the dawn song are two places in the dramatic action where the pattern is most visually dramatized. The imagery of the stars is part of this pattern. The clearest expression of the imagery of light and darkness is in the lightning image that Juliet first uses for their love in the balcony scene. This image of sudden brilliant light in darkness is one of the best visual expressions of the intensity in the love of Romeo and Juliet.

The lightning image leads to a second important image pattern: the explosion imagery. This explosion imagery is related to the larger light-dark pattern. Like the lightning, it merely expresses the violence of that pattern. But Shakespeare is so precise about his use of explosion imagery that it needs to be examined separately. There are only three places in the play where the explosion image is spelled out, although it is clearly implied in other places. The first of these occurs in the last scene of Act II, when Friar Laurence scolds the overanxious Romeo:

> These violent delights have violent ends
> And in their triumph die, like fire and powder,
> Which as they kiss consume:

The second also occurs in Friar Laurence's cell, when Romeo has thrown himself on the floor in despair. In the friar's long speech, he accuses Romeo of abusing, among other things, his wit or intelligence, with the result that his reason:

> Like powder in a skilless soldier's flask,
> Is set afire by thine own ignorance.
> And thou dismembered with thine own defence.

The last of these explosion images is Romeo's. It occurs when he is speaking to the apothecary, and its use implies that Romeo knows the violence he is bringing upon himself in passionate surrender to his melancholy. Romeo hopes that he may die quickly:

> And that the trunk may be discharged of breath
> As violently as hasty powder fired
> Doth hurry from the fatal cannon's womb.

The third dominant image pattern is the death-marriage imagery. Juliet referred to her grave as her wedding bed in the first moments after her encounter with Romeo at the Capulet feast. Later, their suicides and Juliet's drugged sleep dramatize this image pattern; Capulet and Paris specifically refer to death as the bridegroom, as does Juliet in her soliloquy before taking the potion. But the great scene is the last, in which death is challenged by Romeo and summoned as he breaks upon the entrance to the Capulet vault. The very scene of the vault is the dramatic visualization of the death-marriage image. Romeo details the effects of death (and their failure to claim Juliet) and finally names death as her lover. Ironically, he performs the wedding rite, with death as lover, in committing the suicide.

Question 30.
Comment on the use of puns in the play.

Answer
Plays on words were popular in Shakespeare's time and were considered as displays of wit and intelligence. They were used in the most serious circumstances, as in Mercutio's dying words, "Ask for me to-morrow and you shall find me a grave man." Mercutio, Benvolio and Romeo use puns in their exchanges of wit much more extensively than the others, though even the servants and musicians use them. Sometimes the puns are far-fetched, as when Romeo says, "What says my conceal'd lady to my cancell'd love?" twisting the sounds of the words to make a true pun. Mercutio's "fashion-mongers, who stand so much in the new form that they cannot sit at ease on the old bench" requires not only different words, but a knowledge of fashions in dress of the time. Even Juliet, in the height of her emotion, plays on the word "division":

Some say the lark makes sweet division;
This doth not so, for she divideth us.
(Act III, Scene 5)

When the servant tells Capulet that he has a head that will find logs, the latter replies, "Thou shalt be my loggerhead." This sort of obvious punning is excusable in playful exchanges of humor.

Question 31.
When and why is prose used in the play?

Answer

Prose is used by the less important characters, the serving-men in the first scene and in Act IV, Scene 2, Peter and the musicians in Act IV, Scene 5, and by Mercutio, Benvolio, Romeo and the nurse in their humorous scenes. But, as soon as the thought becomes more elevated, or the tone rises, they resort to verse. Even Balthasar, the watchman, and Paris' page speak in verse in the last scene because the tone throughout the scene is elevated.

That more than half the play is in rhyme may be accounted for by the fact that Shakespeare was experimenting when he wrote it. His style had not yet become free or daring, as it was to become later. Furthermore, the play has, to a large extent, the character of a lyric poem, and rhyming verse is the appropriate medium for lyric poetry.